JUNIOR
TENNIS

JUNIOR
TENNIS

MARK VALE

Bounty
Books

PUBLISHER'S NOTE

On the majority of occasions players have been referred to as 'he' in the book. This is simply for convenience and in no way reflects an opinion that tennis is a male-only sport. The text has been written from the point-of-view of teaching a right-handed player. Reverse the advice given for left-handed players to read 'left' for 'right' and vice versa.

First published in Great Britain in 2002 by
Hamlyn, a division of Octopus Publishing Group Ltd

This edition published 2004 by Bounty Books,
a division of Octopus Publishing Group Ltd
2–4 Heron Quays, London E14 4JP

Copyright © Octopus Publishing Group Ltd 2002

ISBN 0 7537 0933 3

A CIP catalogue record for this book is available from the British Library

Printed and bound in China

INTRODUCTION
FOR PARENTS AND JUNIORS

Tennis is one of the most popular and far-reaching sports in the world. Go to any country, from Azerbaijan to Zaire, from Antigua to Zimbabwe, and you are sure to stumble across a tennis court sooner or later.

Tennis is equally popular with men and women, and with boys and girls. You can start playing as soon as you can walk, and you can carry on playing until old age. One man in Denmark is still playing regularly at the grand age of 101. You can play in a wheelchair, and there is a professional tour for wheelchair tennis players.

Tennis is also a sport that requires very little by way of equipment. A racket and a ball are all that is needed to play the game at a basic level. Even if you don't have access to a tennis court and have no opponent to play against, you can always hit the ball against a brick wall.

Beginners often find tennis a tricky and frustrating sport, but as soon as a player hits his or her first crisp, clean shot they realize why so many people are so passsionate about the game. This book will help junior coaches and their pupils to appreciate the joy of tennis. It provides information on everything from where to play and how to get the best out of tennis equipment, to tactics, etiquette and how to develop the confidence to win matches.

There are many different ways of coaching and playing tennis. The instructions in this book are clear and simple, offering a grounding in the basics of the sport, but to progress to the higher levels of the sport players should also invest in lessons from a qualified coach. Young players must appreciate that better tennis only comes with greater practice.

Junior Tennis is structured to give young players easy access to the different aspects of the sport, from its history to tactics and how and when to play each shot.

All About Tennis includes a brief history of the game, details of the four major tournaments that make up the Grand Slam, and a guide to tennis resources on the internet.

Equipment, Courts and Etiquette looks at the equipment and clothing tennis players use and wear and offers advice on choosing the best for junior players. It also explains the different court surfaces and which type of game is best suited to each, the layout of the court, the rules of the game and how it is scored, as well as the standards of behaviour expected of players.

Practical Advice covers how to look for a tennis club that encourages youngsters and how to choose the right coach, the basics of competitive tennis and how to cope with injuries.

Starting Out looks at the final details before a junior actually hits a ball: warming up, how to hold the racket and the purpose of knocking up before a game.

Serve and Return explains the fundamentals of tactics and strategies and choice of shot, whether to stay back or to go to the net. Drills are included to help players to make such decisions second nature.

Once the basics of tactics are understood, the reader moves on to the different shots and how to get such details as grip and stance correct in order to make improvements to the junior's basic game.

The Forehand examines the different shots: the basic groundstroke, the volley, the lob, the dropshot and the smash and how and when to use each to suit the tactics already learned.

The Backhand shows how to get the different shots – the basic groundstroke, the volley and the lob – to work, as well as how to put slice on to a ball and discusses the advantages and disadvantages of using the double-handed backhand.

Doubles looks at this most enjoyable form of the game: the differences between singles and doubles, co-operating with a partner and how to adapt the skills already acquired to it.

Off-court Practice gives a number of drills that juniors can use to improve their skills, judgement, hand-eye co-ordination and general levels of fitness.

Finally, a fun **Quiz** checks how much the junior has learned.

9

ALL ABOUT TENNIS

There are thousands of tennis professionals, but it is the elite players, such as Pete Sampras, Andre Agassi, Martina Hingis, Tim Henman and the Williams sisters, who often inspire youngsters to take up the game. And why not? For those who reach the pinnacle of professional tennis the rewards are immense. The top players travel the world, earn big money and enjoy celebrity status. So the message to all aspiring Agassis and wannabe Williamses is clear: Grab a racket and a ball and get out there and play.

WHERE TO PLAY

Most large towns have at least one tennis club where players can enjoy competitive tennis and structured coaching. In some countries, including Britain, France, Germany, the USA and Australia, tennis is so popular that even smaller towns have a tennis club. But before paying to join one it's a good idea for youngsters to play on public courts just to get the hang of the game. Municipal parks often have tennis courts that are relatively inexpensive to hire.

Tennis is regarded as a summer or 'fair weather' sport, but dedicated players will play even when it is very cold outside. As long as it is not raining or too windy players can still enjoy a fun game. In countries with harsh winters, keen players hone their skills in indoor tennis centres during the colder months.

Opposite: Since being injured a few years ago, Monica Seles has had to adapt her game in order to be competitive once again.

Left: Your local tennis centre may not look as impressive as this, but most towns have at least one court available to the public.

THE HISTORY AND ORIGINS OF TENNIS

Two Englishmen, Major Henry Gem and Major Walter Wingfield, invented tennis in 1858. The two Majors marked out lines on a patch of lawn in Edgbaston, Birmingham, England, and called it a 'lawn tennis court'. For several centuries before that, monks and members of European royalty had played a version of a game now known as 'real tennis' on enclosed courts that resembled abbey cloisters. It was not until Gem and Wingfield collaborated in the mid-19th century that tennis moved outside and onto grass.

The first lawn tennis courts were shaped like an hourglass, i.e. wider at the baseline than at the net. In 1874 Major Wingfield applied to patent his new sport under the title *New and Improved Court for Playing the Ancient Game of Tennis*. He referred to the sport as 'Sphairistike', but soon opted for a term that was much easier to pronounce: 'lawn tennis'.

The game soon became popular with the Victorian aristocracy, who often played it at garden parties. By May 1875 lawn tennis had become so widespread that players decided it was time to lay down proper rules for the sport. The Marylebone Cricket Club, which already governed the rules of real tennis, issued a code of rules, the basis of which is still used to this day.

In the same year, the All England Croquet Club in Wimbledon, south-west London, introduced lawn tennis to its members. Two years later, on Monday 9 July 1877, the world's most famous tennis club held its first championships. A 27-year-old surveyor called Spencer Gore was the first champion. However, it was not until 1884 that women were allowed to compete at Wimbledon.

Slowly but surely, lawn tennis became popular throughout the world. In 1881, the first Championships were held in the USA. Ten years later came the first French Championships, and in 1905 came the inaugural Australian Championships. Nowadays, along with Wimbledon, these three events (the US Open, the French Open and the Australian Open) are collectively known as tennis's Grand Slams. The game's international team competition for men, the Davis Cup, has been running since 1900.

The sport of lawn tennis dropped the word 'lawn' from its name decades ago, partly because courts can now be constructed out of a variety of materials (see pages 26–9). Nowadays the sport is so widespread that most nations in the world has its own tennis association. The International Tennis Federation has nearly 200 member nations, and the ATP (the male players' union) and WTA (the female players' union) have players from more than 100 countries. Tennis is now unquestionably one of the most popular sports in the world.

Opposite: France's Rene Lacoste, who dominated French tennis in the 1920s, winning Wimbledon in 1925 and 1928.

Left: The athletic Suzanne Lenglen, from France, who won Wimbledon six times between 1919 and 1925, was the first superstar champion of women's tennis.

MAJOR TOURNAMENTS

The most important professional tournaments in tennis are the four annual Grand Slams. January sees the Australian Open, which is held at Melbourne Park in Melbourne. In late May and early June there is the French Open, hosted at Roland Garros in Paris. Late June and early July is the highlight of the tennis calendar. It is the time when the top players flock to the All England Club in Wimbledon for the tournament technically known as 'The Championships', but commonly referred to as 'Wimbledon'. The final Grand Slam of the year is the US Open at Flushing Meadows in New York in late August–early September.

Besides these majors, which feature both male and female players, hundreds of lesser grade tennis tournaments help to make up the men's ATP (Association of Tennis Professionals) Tour and the women's WTA (Women's Tennis Association) Tour. Some of the more important events feature both men and women, but the majority are single sex tournaments.

ATP and WTA tournaments are held all over the world, bringing top-class tennis to venues in such unlikely locations as Uzbekistan, Indonesia and Qatar. Both the men's and the women's tours culminate in a year-end championship for all the top players.

The professionals also compete in international team tournaments. In the men's game there is the hugely popular Davis Cup, which is a league event played throughout the year and all over the world. Teams have to progress up through the leagues into the elite World Group, the winner of which is declared the Davis Cup champion nation. For the women there is the Fed Cup, which is run along similar lines to the Davis Cup. There are not as many nations competing in the women's event, but it is just as hotly contested.

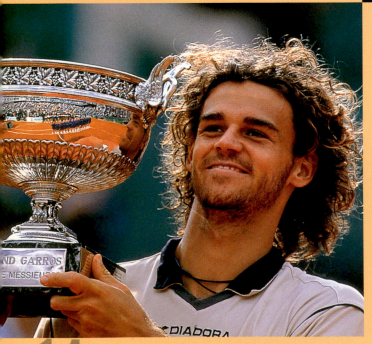

Top: Venus Williams is one half of the superb American duo, the Williams sisters, who have won many tournaments between them.

Left: Brazil's Gustavo Kuerten is one of the most recognizable sportsmen in South America.

TENNIS ON THE INTERNET

The Internet is an ideal medium for sports fans because news, results and comments can be posted onto websites instantly. There are thousands of tennis websites, many of them dedicated to news and results; others are attached to player fan clubs, while some offer information on racket and clothing shops, coaching and tennis holidays. The good thing about the World Wide Web is that it is constantly changing and developing. However, as a result of this perpetual evolution, it is impossible to produce an exhaustive list of tennis sites. The best thing to do is to search the Internet using one of the many widely available search engines, but to get you started here are some of the best and most popular tennis websites:

NEWS AND RESULTS

There are hundreds of websites offering news and results from tennis tournaments. You can't go wrong with the two official sites for the men's and women's tours:

www.atptennis.com
www.wtatour.com

The above sites include extensive information and statistics on the professional players, but if you just want results you should try www.stevegtennis.com, which often seems to have match scores quicker than the official websites.

Most larger tournaments have their own sites (e.g. www.wimbledon.com, www.usopen.org, www.ausopen.org, www.frenchopen.org). These sites contain facts, scores and statistics, and some also contain advice on how to buy tournament tickets.

PLAYER FANCLUBS

Fan club websites are popular throughout the world of sport and tennis is no exception. Many of the sites are professionally produced and officially endorsed ... others are less impressive. Try these for starters:

www.mhingis.com
www.kournikova.com
www.gugakuerten.com.br
www.thewilliamssisters.com

EQUIPMENT AND KIT

There are many bargains to be found when buying equipment and kit on the Internet. American sites are the market leaders, but if you live outside the USA delivery costs can be prohibitive.

www.tennis-warehouse.com
www.golfandtennisworld.com
www.e-rackets.com
www.LTA.org.uk/onlineshop
www.pwp.com

COACHING

Most of the tennis instruction sites are based in the USA. This isn't entirely surprising, given that there are more American players in the world's top 100 than any other nation. Try these websites for coaching tips:

www.tennisone.com
www.tennis.com
www.aproch.com

NATIONAL GOVERNING BODIES

Many national governing bodies have websites with useful links to clubs, coaches and coaching, schools tennis, advice for beginners and regional and national competitions. Among them are:

www.fft.fr
www.tennis.se
www.usta.com
www.lta.org.uk
www.tennis.org.nz
www.satennis.co.za
www.tennis-aus.com.au
www.federtennis.systex.it
www.dansktennisforbund.dk
www.deutschertennisbund.com
www.canoe.ca/SlamTennisCanada

EQUIPMENT, COURTS AND ETIQUETTE

Players do not need to spend vast amounts of money on clothing and equipment to enjoy the game of tennis. All that is needed is a racket, balls, tennis shoes and suitable attire. Of course, for those players more concerned with sartorial elegance than with skill and fitness, there is still great potential to spend heavily on the latest kit and meaningless paraphernalia.

TENNIS BALLS

The item of tennis equipment that players buy most often is the humble tennis ball. However, players should not be tempted to go for the cheapest option. More expensive, higher quality balls are usually worth the extra money as they will not only last longer but also bounce better.

There are two main types of tennis ball on the market: pressurized balls and pressureless balls. All professional players and many amateur players use pressurized balls (the ones that come in a sealed tube with gas inside it), despite the fact that these balls go softer more quickly than pressureless balls. Pressurized balls are easier to control and have more 'feel' on the strings of the racket than pressureless balls, which are harder and bounce off the strings more quickly.

The other significant ball on the market is the new bigger tennis ball. At the time of writing, these balls are still being tested and are not in use on the professional circuit.

Opposite: The basic equipment needed for tennis includes racket, balls, shoes, clothing and of course a bag to hold everything in.

RACKETS

Buying a tennis racket can be a daunting proposition for the uninitiated. Upon entering a sports shop, the novice or junior player is confronted by rows and rows of colourful, expensive and seemingly sophisticated rackets, each apparently offering the solution to the flaws in his game ... but which one to choose?

There is of course some correlation between price and value, i.e. the more you pay, the better the racket. But this is not the whole story. Players should concern themselves with finding a racket that is appropriate for their needs and which also feels comfortable in the hand.

Players who are serious about their tennis should consider spending as much as they can afford, but it is also important for them to get a racket that is correct for their standard of play. A specialist racket shop will be able to offer advice for most budgets and needs.

There are essentially five major types of tennis racket: inexpensive rackets; beginners' or improvers' rackets; club players' rackets; professional rackets; and junior rackets.

1. RACKET FRAME: modern rackets are made of graphite, carbon or a combination of light but strong composite materials.
2. BUMPER STRIP: the very top of a racket frame is covered in a strip of plastic that prevents damage to the racket when it is scraped on the surface of the court.
3. STRINGS: racket strings are made of nylon or similar man-made materials (very occasionally sheep gut). The vertical strings are called main strings, while the horizontal strings are called cross strings.
4. GROMMETS: these are the small plastic sheaths through which the strings are threaded.
5. VIBRATION DAMPENER: this piece of rubber prevents vibrations in the racket head from moving down into the player's arm. It can help prevent tennis elbow.
6. THROAT: the area between the racket head and the handle.
7. HANDLE: this comes in a variety of thicknesses
8. GRIP: this covers the handle and provides a soft, tacky connection between hand and racket.
9. BUTT: the base of the racket handle.

INEXPENSIVE RACKETS
Should be avoided because they don't allow players to progress and improve. Suitable for a casual game of tennis in a municipal park, but not for anybody with competitive aspirations.

GOOD BEGINNERS' OR IMPROVERS' RACKETS
Invariably these are the most technically advanced. They are designed to help players iron out (or disguise) the technical deficiencies in their game. They often have very thick frames (in order to help cut down vibration on off-centre hits and increase power on shots) and extra large heads (in order to give novices a bigger hitting area on the strings). Sometimes rackets of this category are extra long in order to give more reach and a better chance of getting the serve in.

CLUB PLAYERS' RACKETS
Designed for regular players who hit the ball well. They can be expensive, but tend to have fewer technological gimmicks than beginners' rackets.

PROFESSIONAL RACKETS
Very basic in design because the people who use them almost always hit the ball perfectly, right in the centre of the strings.

JUNIOR RACKETS
Most brands offer a selection of junior rackets, which are smaller, shorter and have thinner grips. Youngsters should be encouraged to start out with junior rackets, but many coaches and parents are keen to move them onto adult rackets quickly in order to avoid the expense of having to buy frequent replacements.

   All players should be encouraged to choose a racket with a correctly sized handle that can be held comfortably. Ideally, when the player puts his playing hand around the grip, there should be one finger's width between the ends of the gripping fingers and the palm. A wrongly-sized grip may cause injuries like tennis elbow.

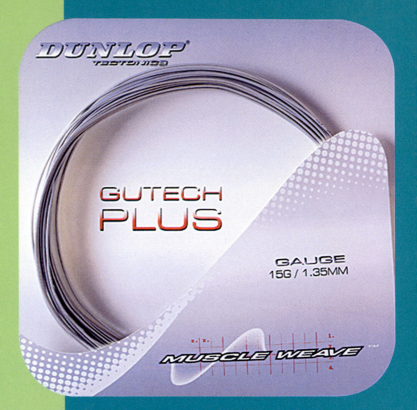

STRINGS AND GRIPS

The importance of good racket strings should not be underestimated. The strings are the part of the racket that makes contact with the ball and, as such, they are crucial to ball control.

Many top players are so acutely aware of the importance of having quality racket strings that they opt to have new rackets restrung immediately upon purchase. This practice is not as bizarre as it seems, because factory strings are often low quality and the racket may have been on the shop shelf for many months. Most racket specialists, tennis clubs and large sports shops offer restringing services.

Good quality strings have about 50 hours of play in them before the accuracy of shots is affected. If a player hits the ball very hard, however, strings may break before the 50 hours are up. Some players who hit the ball softly can play for months without breaaking the strings, but eventually they will start to notice a drop in performance. Similarly, if a racket isn't used for several months the tension of the strings will slacken.

STRING TENSION

Beginners can get confused when a racket stringer asks what tension they would like their racket strung at. As a general rule, lower tensions offer more power and less control, while higher tensions offer more control and less power. If a player requires more power than control, rackets should be strung at 40 to 55 pounds. For a combination of power and control (the best option for beginners), 50 to 60 pounds is ideal. For control rather than power, 60 to 70 pounds is appropriate. These are only rough estimates, as a professional racket stringer will take into consideration the size of racket head and the materials used in the frame.

STRING SAVERS

Some players choose to use string savers. These are small pieces of plastic inserted where the horizontal and vertical strings cross. They increase the life of racket strings by stopping them from rubbing against one another and wearing thin.

Opposite: Racket strings are made of man-made materials like nylon or, occasionally, sheep gut.

Right: Vibration dampeners can help prevent tennis elbow.

VIBRATION DAMPENERS

Many players insert a small piece of rubber between the lowest horizontal string and the throat of the racket, although they can be placed anywhere outside the cross-strung area of the racket. This so-called 'vibration dampener' prevents the racket from juddering too much when the ball is hit. The use of a vibration dampener not only gives a smoother, cleaner strike but also helps to avoid tennis elbow, since it stops shock waves travelling down the racket into the joints in the player's arm.

GRIPS

The grip of the racket, which is wrapped around the handle, is more important than many people think. It is the connection between player and racket, and it can affect control markedly. Grip material should absorb sweat from the palm and give the player a comfortable handhold on the racket.

There are two types of grip available. Firstly there are 'replacement grips', basically a thick piece of material that wraps directly onto the racket handle after the old grip has worn out. Secondly, players can opt for an 'overgrip', which is wrapped on top of the original or replacement grip to make it slightly bigger or to provide a non-slip hold. It is critical that players buy a racket with the correctly sized handle. When the player closes his hand over the grip, there should be a finger's width between the ends of the gripping fingers and the palm. If the handle is too small it can be built up with an overgrip. The wrong size grip will affect the player's shots and can cause tennis elbow.

Above and left: Grips allow players to keep a secure, comfortable hold on the racket.

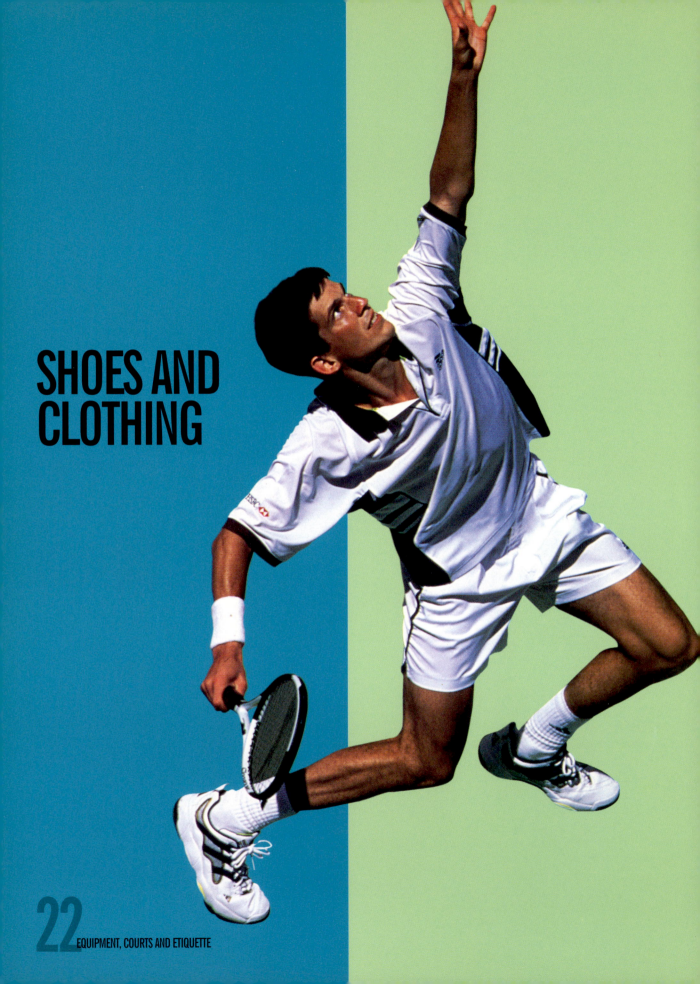

SHOES AND CLOTHING

TENNIS SHOES

Good tennis players move about the court in all directions throughout the match, so they need high quality footwear that is both light and supportive.

Players should be advised to buy tennis-specific shoes because all other footwear, including running shoes, is not designed for the sideways movement involved in playing tennis. The wrong footwear will almost certainly cause blisters and may lead to serious foot injuries. Very few sports shops stock a wide selection of tennis-specific shoes, so players may find they have to visit a specialist shop to get the best shoes.

Many tennis players drag their toes when they serve, and unless this part of the shoe is fortified it will quickly wear out. Most of the world's tennis courts are hard, so tennis shoes must have cushioning support on the heel and sole to aid mobility and help prevent injury. Players should take care to choose a sole pattern that is suitable for the type of court surface they play on. Some hard court or clay court shoes have a herringbone pattern on the sole, grass court shoes have tiny plastic studs, and indoor carpet tennis shoes have smooth soles. Players who play on a variety of surfaces, but who don't wish to buy a separate pair of shoes for each, should opt for hard court shoes, which are the most versatile. However, more exclusive clubs with indoor carpet courts may insist that players wear indoor shoes.

TENNIS SHIRTS

Many modern, expensive tennis shirts are made of special wicking fabrics that draw moisture away from the player's body as he sweats. Good quality tennis shirts should also have a collar that can be turned up to protect the player's neck from the sun. Buttons or a zip around the throat will provide further temperature control.

The colour of the shirt isn't really that important, although white kit is cooler in the summer and disguises sweat patches better than dark kit. However, some tennis clubs still insist that their members wear 'predominantly white clothing', although this tradition is rapidly dying out.

TENNIS SHORTS

A good pair of tennis shorts should be baggy enough to allow freedom of movement as the player runs and stretches around the court. Pockets must be big enough to hold a spare ball. Many shorts for men now come with an inner-pant lining; if not, cycling shorts or a sports underpants should be combined with the shorts.

TENNIS SKIRTS AND DRESSES

Tennis skirts and dresses are still a popular choice for female players. They allow freedom of movement and have shorts attached, complete with pockets for balls, when serving.

Skirts and dresses come in a variety of styles and colours. Current fashion is for short hemlines and bright colours. However, as with shirts and shorts, some tennis clubs may insist upon more traditional, white clothing.

TENNIS KITBAGS

A kitbag helps players keep all their tennis gear together in one place. The bag should be long enough to accommoodate at least two rackets (serious players will always go to a match with at least two rackets in case they break the strings of one in mid-match), a pair of shoes and clothing. Separate pockets for damp kit and for valuables are useful too.

SOCKS

Tennis socks need to be thick enough in order to absorb sweat and provide ankle support, but not so thick that they compromise the fit of the player's tennis shoes.

Opposite: The rigours of professional tennis mean that players need hard-wearing tennis-specific shoes and clothing that 'wicks' away the sweat during play.

Right: The net should be at the correct height (0.914m or 3ft from the ground in the middle) before you play. Many clubs provide measuring sticks.

THE COURT AND THE NET

THE COURT

Tennis courts have a variety of surfaces and are maintained to varying standards, but one thing they all share is identical dimensions.

The official measurements of a tennis court are 23.77m (78ft) long and 8.23m (27ft) wide. For doubles the sidelines along either side of the court are used, thus increasing the court width to 10.97m (36ft). The construction of the court will affect the speed of the court and the bounce of the ball.

COURT CONSTRUCTION	SPEED	BOUNCE
clay	slow	high
shale	slow	high
tarmac	medium	medium
concrete	medium	medium/high
acrylic	medium	medium
artificial grass	fast	low
carpet	fast	low
plastic tiles	fast	low
grass	fast	low

NB The player's style of play will have some effect on the bounce of the ball and its speed off the surface.

THE NET

Players should be encouraged to check the height of the net before they play, some tennis clubs provide a measuring stick – which is usually found hanging from a net post – for this purpose. At the very middle (where players should measure it), the net should be 0.914m (3ft) from the ground, and at the sides it will be slightly higher. As players gain experience they will learn to recognize if the net is at the correct height.

24

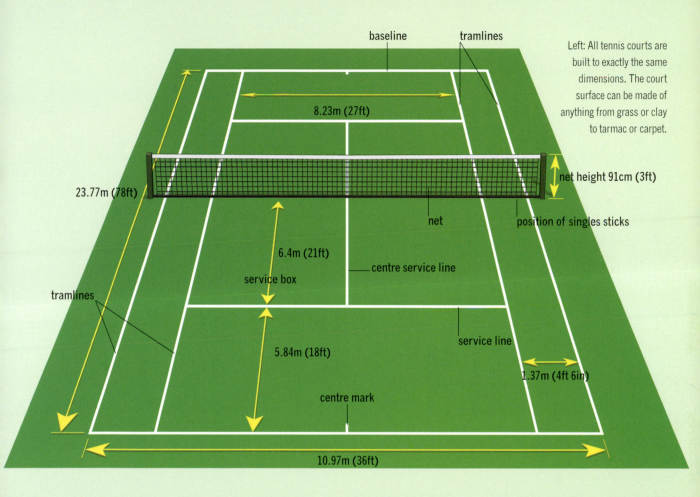

baseline   tramlines

8.23m (27ft)

Left: All tennis courts are built to exactly the same dimensions. The court surface can be made of anything from grass or clay to tarmac or carpet.

net height 91cm (3ft)

23.77m (78ft)

net

position of singles sticks

6.4m (21ft)

centre service line

service box

5.84m (18ft)

service line

tramlines

1.37m (4ft 6in)

centre mark

10.97m (36ft)

THE SINGLES STICKS

Most courts in the world are marked out as doubles courts (i.e. with tramlines down both sides). According to the rules, during singles play the net should be supported between the tramlines with what are known as 'singles sticks'. The use of singles sticks prevents players from hitting very low shots down the lines. In practice, however, amateur players seldom bother using singles sticks.

The singles sticks should be positioned 0.914m (3ft) from the singles tramline out towards the doubles tramline and they ensure that the net is the correct height at the singles tramline.

ANATOMY OF A TENNIS COURT

To the uninitiated, the markings on a tennis court can seem complicated; however, most junior players seem to quickly grasp the essentials of the court layout.

The lines on the court should be between 2.5cm (1in) and 5cm (2in) thick, except for the baselines, which are 10cm (4in) thick. The lines separate the court into different sections, some of which are for general play, others for serving into.

In doubles, players use the whole court, including the tramlines. In singles the areas between the tramlines are not part of the court, so if the ball lands in them it is 'out'. In both doubles and singles, players serve from behind the baseline into the diagonally opposite service box. If the ball doesn't land in the correct service box the serve is not allowed. Players are never allowed to serve into the tramlines.

COURT SURFACES

Above left: Gustavo Kuerten
(receiving) and Wayne Ferreira
(serving) battle it out on a hard court
in Indianapolis.

Above right: Roland Garros is home to
the biggest and best-known clay
court tournament.

HARD COURTS

The vast majority of tennis courts around the world
are what is known as 'hard courts'. Hard courts can be
constructed out of tarmac, concrete, acrylic, or any
other suitable material. They require considerable
work to lay down but once in place, they need virtually
no maintenance except regular sweeping.

The best thing about playing on hard courts is that,
unless they are the old, cracked tarmac ones, which
are frequently found in public parks, the bounce is
almost always true. Of all court surfaces, hard courts
most favour the all-round player. Whether a player is a
baseline specialist or likes to play from the net, hard
courts offer no special advantage. To win on this
surface players must vary their serve, because the ball
bounces so consistently that opponents will soon get
used to it and return with power. Players should also
try to put volleys much deeper towards the baseline,
and should generally keep groundstrokes low, this is

because many hard courts give the ball a very high bounce. If a player fails to keep the ball low, his opponent will be able to return hard and fast past him.

The main disadvantage of hard courts is that they have unforgiving surfaces that can take their toll on player's legs and, in particular joints, if they play on them regularly.

CLAY COURTS

Clay courts are generally made from the same clay as housebricks. They are popular in countries with hot climates, but because they require so much skill to build and maintain, they are expensive and normally found only in exclusive clubs.

Of all the tennis court surfaces, clay is the slowest and therefore gives players most time to line up and hit the ball. It is very hard to hit outright winners on clay, and players who do the best on this surface are fit baseliners who favour long drawn-out rallies.

The trick is for players to keep putting pressure on their opponents from the baseline, waiting for the right moment before moving in for the kill. Dropshots are particularly effective on clay because opponents are invariably at the baseline and because, with lots of backspin, the ball will bounce much lower and softer than on other surfaces. Regular clay players must work hard on their fitness as rallies are much longer. A typical three-set match can last for three hours on clay. Players should also practise sliding on clay because, unlike on hard courts where players have to keep their feet planted on the ground when striking the ball, on clay players can slide into the shot because the surface is loose. Clay is less harsh on the legs than hard courts.

GRASS COURTS

Grass is, of course, the surface used at Wimbledon and many of the other mid-summer tournaments in Britain, where it is very popular, but throughout the rest of the world it is a rare surface. Many consider it outdated and impractical because it requires so much maintenance.

In theory, a very basic grass court is the easiest and cheapest to build. All that is needed is a flat lawn, a heavy roller, some paint for the lines and a tennis net. This is fine for players who aren't fussy about unpredictable ball bounces, but for a decent court surface, a lot of money and time must be spent on maintenance. At some upmarket tennis clubs, the groundsmen spend all year looking after the grass courts, even though they are only used for four months out of twelve.

When the ball bounces on grass it skids off very fast and very low. It is a surface that favours players who like to serve and volley, and who are happiest at the net. Baseline players find that they simply cannot attack serves with confidence on grass, because the ball bounces so low. The serves skim off the grass so fast that it becomes extremely hard to put back a return with any power. Players who serve hard and fast and then immediately run to the net for the volley are almost always the ones who win on grass. It is a soft, natural surface and therefore causes less damage to the legs and joints than hard courts.

INDOOR COURTS

Players lucky enough to have access to an indoor court are usually unconcerned by what the surface is. Normally indoor tennis centres have hard acrylic courts or carpet courts. At some indoor tournament venues they even use plastic tiles to make up the court. Indoor courts cost much more to hire than outdoor courts; this is because they are costly to build and are expensive to heat and light. But when it is cold and rainy outside players have little alternative but to move inside.

ARTIFICIAL GRASS

Artificial grass is becoming very popular in Britain for tennis because it is durable, needs little maintenance and is softer on the joints than hard courts. However, there are virtually no professional tournaments played on this surface.

When it is brand new, artificial grass has a good grip, like firm clay, and favours baseliners. However, over time as the plastic blades become flattened and worn, the surface becomes much slicker and favours the serve and volleyer. If a player falls over on artificial grass he will invariably end up with a painful friction burn.

UNUSUAL SURFACES

There is nothing to stop a tennis club or centre building a tennis court out of any material whatsoever. There is one tennis centre in Bombay in India that has courts made of cow manure. Every morning the groundsmen lay fresh dung on the courts and roll it flat. Apparently the smell is not too bad.

In Australia it is not unknown to play on courts made of crushed anthills, and in Finland every winter an ice tennis tournament is held on a court marked out on an ice rink. However, players are required to bring their own ice skates.

Left: Indoor courts will have a variety of surfaces, ranging from hard acrylic to plastic tiles.

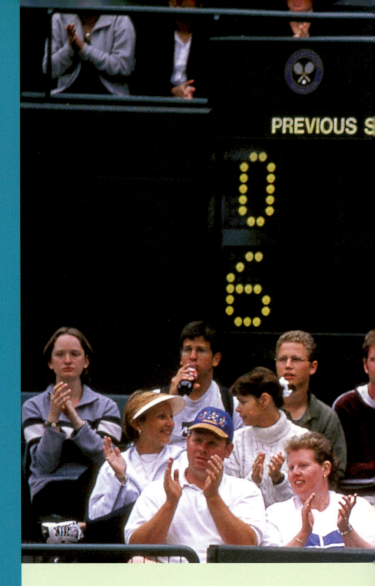

Right: The first player to win six games (by a margin of at least two games over their opponent) wins the set. Matches normally consist of the best of three or five sets.

RULES AND SCORING

The rules of tennis can seem complicated and obscure to the newcomer. But after a little guidance from parent or coach, most youngsters soon grasp the fundamentals.

TENNIS FUNDAMENTALS

The game of tennis is simple, in principle. Points are accrued by winning rallies, which begin when one player serves to the other. Each player must alternately get the ball back over the net (before it bounces twice) and into the opponent's side of the court. The first player to fail in this objective loses the point. Players are allowed to volley the ball or let it bounce once, but they must let serves bounce once before striking the ball. This sounds straightforward enough, but there are several key rules that complicate things, and which all players should understand.

5.53 ROLEX .35

SETS   GAMES

MISS M. WEINGARTNER

v

MISS M. SELES

0 0

2 6

KEY RULES

1 A player serving must keep his feet behind the baseline before striking the ball. If the baseline is touched the service is deemed a foul serve.

2 The rules do not oblige players to serve overarm, but players will not be competitive unless they do.

3 Players have two chances to get their serve in – in other words they are permitted one foul serve. If the ball hits the net and bounces in, then the point must be replayed. This does not count as a foul serve.

4 If the ball hits the net during a normal rally and bounces in then the players simply play on.

5 If the ball lands on a boundary line of the court it is considered 'in'.

6 When a player hits the ball he must only strike it once, cleanly with his racket. Unintentional double hits are allowed, but intentional ones are not.

7 If, while the ball is still in play, a player touches the net with racket, clothing or body, the offending player loses the point.

8 Players are not allowed to lean over the net to play the ball, except where backspin or strong wind causes the ball to bounce on their side of the net and then go back over to their opponent's side before it has bounced again.

9 According to the rules, if the ball lands on a stray ball during play, the rally should continue; even if the ball has bounced in an awkward way.

SCORING

Before commencing a match, players should agree on how many sets they are going to play. Normally juniors play the best of three sets (i.e. the first to win two sets). To win a set players need to win six games by a margin of at least two games. If the score gets to six games all, most players agree to play a tiebreak.

To win a game a player needs to win four points before his opponent, again by a margin of at least two points. When a player has no points his score is called 'love'. With one point, his score is 15, at two points it's 30, at three points it's 40, and after four points the game is won. If both players reach 40 the score is 'deuce'. Either player must now win two points in a row (after one point they are said to have the 'advantage') to win the game. If one player has the advantage but loses the next point the score returns to deuce.

CHANGING ENDS

Players change ends after they have played one game and then change again after every alternate game. The practice of changing ends is employed to avoid one player enjoying an advantage (the wind or sun might be better at one end, for example) throughout the match.

CHOOSING WHO STARTS

To decide who serves first and who plays at which end, players usually 'spin the racket'. Tossing a coin would be equally effective, but players rarely have coins available when out on the court.

Most players will ask their opponent 'Up or down?' before spinning their racket on its head and letting it fall onto the ground. The racket is picked up and the logo on the butt of the racket's handle examined. If the logo is the right way up, the person who called 'Up' can choose which end to play or whether to serve. If it is the wrong way up then the person who called 'Down' gets to choose.

If the winner of the spin chooses to serve first, then the other player chooses which end to receive first. A player who wins the spin may decide to receive serve first in an attempt to break the opponent's serve and gain an early advantage. If the winner of the spin chooses which end to play from first, then the other player chooses whether to serve or receive first.

SERVING

At the start of each game the server must stand behind the baseline on the right-hand side of the centre mark. He must strike his first serve diagonally into the left-hand (or 'deuce') service box on the other side of the net. The server has two chances to get his serve into the correct service box. If the player fails on both occasions the serve is called a 'double fault' and the point is won by the receiver. After each point has been played, the server alternates between the left-hand ('deuce') and right-hand ('advantage') service boxes of his opponent.

PLAYING A TIEBREAK

If the score reaches six games all, most players agree to play a tiebreak. The player whose turn it is to serve plays the first point. He serves one point to the left-hand court. His opponent then serves two points, serving the first one to the right-hand court. From then on players serve two points alternately (starting by serving to the wrong side each time) until one player reaches seven points (with a margin of at least two points). Players should change ends after every six points. In doubles, players serve the tiebreak out in the normal serving order. Some tiebreaks can go on for a very long time. One of the longest was played between Bjorn Borg and Premjit Lal at Wimbledon in 1973. The score between Borg and Lal reached an amazing 20–18.

Right: It's important to respect your opponent and be gracious in victory or defeat.

ETIQUETTE

TENNIS ETIQUETTE

In addition to the rules of tennis, there are a number of other practices and customs that should be respected by all players. Tennis relies greatly on its code of etiquette or unwritten rules, which help maintain a sporting balance within the game. If players ignore tennis etiquette they will be regarded as rude and unsporting.

PUNCTUALITY

Players should aim to arrive at least 15 minutes before the start of a match. They will then have time to warm up and get all their kit ready. Tennis courts can be expensive to hire so it is important not to be late.

CLOTHING

Some exclusive clubs insist that players wear predominantly white clothing. Even at clubs without such stringent dress codes, players should be encouraged to wear clean, recognized tennis kit. Good kit helps project an image of confidence and competence, and it is also considered a mark of respect to an opponent.

THE KNOCK-UP

All tennis matches should be preceded by a five-minute knock-up. During this time players hit gentle shots to ease themselves into playing before the point scoring starts.

RETURNING STRAY BALLS

It is polite for an opponent to send stray balls back to the server's end between points. The player should shout 'ball coming' to warn the server that a ball is on its way back. He should not, however, send balls back during a point. If, for example, a first serve goes out, the receiver should hit the ball back into the net, or catch it and put it into his pocket. The receiver should resist the temptation to practise his return of serve by drilling the ball back.

LINE CALLING

It is customary for the player whose side of the court the ball lands in to state clearly if it was out. If, however, the two players disagree, they should agree to play the point again.

ACKNOWLEDGING EXCELLENCE AND GOOD FORTUNE

If a player hits an exceptionally good shot, his opponent should acknowledge it by telling him or clapping. By the same token, if a player wins a point with a lucky shot that clips the net and dribbles into the opponent's court, the fortuitous player should apologize.

RESPECT OTHER MATCHES

Players should never march onto a court while others are playing on it – even if they have arrived late for a court they have booked. Instead, they should wait for the point or game in progress to finish. Similarly, if players have to cross another occupied court to get to theirs, they should wait until the players have finished their point and should walk around the back of the court. Furthermore, if a player accidentally hits a ball onto a neighbouring occupied court he should wait until the players have finished their point before asking, politely, for the ball to be returned.

NEW BALLS

Before serving with brand new balls, the server should always hold up the ball to his opponent so that the receiver can clearly see that a new can of balls has been started.

SENSIBLE NOT DANGEROUS PLAY

If a player at the net gives an opponent a really easy shot to return, the second player should not hit the ball hard straight back at him. To do so is not against the rules, but it is both unsporting and dangerous. In addition, players should warn their opponents if they spot a stray ball rolling around on the other side of the court. If a player unwittingly steps on a stray ball he could be injured.

Opposite: Always hold up new balls to show your opponent before you serve.
Opposite below: It's polite to acknowledge when your opponent plays a very skilful shot.

Right: Always clear away empty ball cans and rubbish from the court at the end of the match.

Below right: Make sure you shut the court gate after play so that other players don't lose their balls through the netting.

CHANGING ENDS

When changing ends, players should walk around the net rather than jump over it.

NO SWEARING OR SHOUTING

Even if players get frustrated with their play, they must never talk or shout during the course of a point because it may put off their opponent. Players should never curse or swear.

MIXED DOUBLES ETIQUETTE

When playing mixed doubles, although it is not against the rules, it is considered unsportsmanlike to hit every ball possible at the weaker player.

UNDERARM WARNING

On the rare occasions (for example, in very windy weather) that players decide to serve underarm, they should warn their opponents. Players who do not will be considered rude.

NATURAL BREAKS

If a player needs to go to the toilet during a match, he should wait until it is time to change ends before excusing himself.

POST-MATCH ETIQUETTE

At the end of the match players should approach the net and shake hands with their opponent. They should also help to pick up all the balls, and clear away any litter beside the court.

GENERAL STRATEGY

It is important for players to be in the right frame of mind when they play a match. Players with excellent technique and shot selection can sometimes lose to opponents who have the mental advantage over them. Recently, top tennis professionals have started employing psychologists as well as coaches and trainers to help their overall game. Here are some general tips on how players can defeat an opponent with psychology.

DEALING WITH CHEATS

In tennis, just as in any other sport, players will occasionally come across opponents who are not entirely honest, downright cheats even. The principal area of cheating is line calling. Players often aim their shots at the edges of the court, so as to force their opponents to move about as much as possible and miss the ball. This means that many balls land on or very close to the lines. Certain unscrupulous players want to win at any cost and if this means making bad line calls then they will do it. How should players react to this injustice?

Firstly, a player should give their opponent the benefit of the doubt, rather than assume he is cheating. He might have made a genuine mistake on the line call. Ask politely if he is sure the ball was out. If convinced that the line call was wrong a player can ask for a let. However, if the ball was on his opponent's side of the net, then technically it is up to him to decide whether it was in or out.

If a player is certain that an opponent is actually cheating and he refuses to grant a let, then the only option left open is to call for an official or a third party. However, under no circumstances should a player actually accuse an opponent of cheating or lose his temper. The best thing to do is to play even better and show that superior skill can overcome bad sportsmanship.

Opposite: If you think your opponent has made an incorrect line call, then at first you should ask them politely if they are sure. If you think they are cheating then call in a third party to adjudicate.

WINDY WEATHER

Strong winds can really buffet the ball and blow it about as a player prepares to make contact. It can also cause a good shot to land out, which can be extremely frustrating. Players should be prepared for the ball to be blown about as they are about to hit it. They must watch it even more carefully than usual, just in case the wind moves it off course at the last second.

If the wind is at a player's back, he will have to take care not to hit the ball long into his opponent's court. He should consider using more topspin or striking the ball less hard to keep it in. On the other hand, when playing into the wind, players can risk hitting the ball harder than usual because the wind will prevent it going long. The wind can also be used to assist a dropshot or a lob if it is blowing in the right direction.

Sometimes, when the wind is really strong, players are best advised to use an underarm serve, rather than run the risk of tossing the ball up for an overarm shot.

BAD WEATHER

Many people regard tennis as a fair weather or summertime sport, but this simply is not the case. People play outside all over the world in different climates and different weather conditions. If players are not lucky enough to have access to indoor courts, then sooner or later they will have to play when it is cold, windy, rainy or extremely hot and humid.

Some players get really put off by adverse weather and try to blame their mistakes on the elements. However, junior players should bear in mind that the weather is exactly the same for them as it is for their opponent. Instead of moaning about it, players should use the peculiarities of the climate to their own advantage.

RAIN

Players should avoid playing in the rain whenever possible. The first priority in such conditions is to wear shoes with good grips, and to take care not to slip on the wet court.

COLD WEATHER

Players must always stretch and warm up their muscles before playing in cold conditions. They should also wear several layers of thin clothing rather than one layer of thick clothing, as this will keep them warmer and allow them to strip off layers as their body heats up. Tracksuits should not be so baggy that they interfere with leg or arm movement.

SUN AND HEAT

Sunglasses or a peaked hat will help curb the glare of the sun as a player serves. By the same token, players should try lobbing their opponent if he will be forced to look into the sun.

Players must make sure that they stay properly hydrated before, during and after tennis, especially if it is a very hot day. Exposed skin should be covered with a sun protection cream, and players should sit in the shade between games. Sometimes there will even be a shady part of the court in which players can briefly shelter between points. Over the course of a long match this type of precaution can make a genuine difference to a player's fitness levels.

MATCH PREPARATION

Some tennis players prepare so well for their matches that they have done much of the hard work before they even step out on court. Here are some tips to ensure that players give themselves the best possible chance of winning.

1 Players should eat well the night before a match, consuming lots of carbohydrates such as pasta, rice and potatoes. They should also drink lots of water but avoid drinks with caffeine, such as cola, coffee and tea.

2 They must get as much sleep as they can.

3 Players should eat a good sized meal before the match (not less than two hours before it starts, though) and hydrate the body with lots of fluids.

4 They should check, and double check, that they have everything they need in their kitbag. Players should take at least two rackets (in case of broken strings), shorts or skirt, tracksuit, shirt, socks, shoes, sweatbands, headwear, balls, high carbohydrate snacks, plenty of water or hydration sports drinks, plasters for blisters and sun protection cream.

5 Players should get to their match venue well before the match is due to start. It is rude to keep an opponent waiting. It is also important to have time to stretch, warm up and knock up properly. If a player has to run straight onto the court as soon as he arrives, he will risk sustaining a muscle injury and is likely to lose the first few games.

PLAYING A TIEBREAK

If a set reaches six games all, the players have to contest a tiebreak to decide who wins the set. It is often the player who remains the coolest under pressure who wins a tiebreak.

Players must remember the scoring and serving system in the tiebreak. The more familiar they are with it, the more comfortable they will feel.

First serves should be played safely, as at this stage of the set it is too risky to go for aces unless the player is leading the tiebreak by a large margin.

Players should pick on any weaknesses they have noticed in their opponent's game. Every point counts in a tiebreak, so players must put as much pressure as they can on their rival.

If a player finds himself losing in a tiebreak situation, then he should think about just one point at a time. He should forget what the score is and concentrate on winning the point that is currently up for grabs. To have any chance, he must remain fully focused and keep calm.

TEMPER CONTROL

Unlike doubles, which is a team game, in singles players have only themselves to blame for any mistakes. When things start to go wrong in tennis it can be extremely frustrating. However, whatever else they do, players must not lose their temper. They must remain calm and focused if they are to get their game back on track.

If you look at the professional game you will notice that more often than not, players who control their temper, even under extreme pressure, are the ones who manage to turn hopeless situations into victories. Just look at Pete Sampras, Steffi Graf and Tim Henman: all extremely calm characters.

It is crucial that players retain their discipline. If a player starts shouting and throwing his racket about, people will notice how flustered he is and take advantage of the situation. When things start to go wrong, players should take a deep breath, forget about the last point and focus on the positive aspects of their game.

Opposite: Controlling your temper will help you to concentrate on your game and will save your equipment from unnecessary damage.

PRACTICAL ADVICE

3

GETTING STARTED

There is no official age at which children should start playing tennis. Some coaches believe that children should play as soon as they can walk, while others prefer to wait until youngsters reach the age of six or seven. If children start too early there is a risk that they might 'burn out' before reaching their teens. However, late-starters may miss out on valuable early-years training, or they may get drawn into another sport.

Pete Sampras started at the age of seven, Andre Agassi first hit a ball aged four and Tim Henman took up tennis aged 30 months. The top women players have a similar variety of starting ages. There is no right answer, and all parents can do is seek guidance from a respected coach, preferably somebody who teaches children. The best advice is to gently introduce children to tennis at first, encouraging them further if they really enjoy the game. Too much pressure at a young age can lead to a complete rejection of the sport.

Most youngsters start playing tennis with their parents. Informal tuition by parents is fine while children are mastering the basic art of hitting the ball and familiarizing themselves with the court, but there will come a point where children require lessons from a qualified coach if they are to progress. Most tennis clubs and tennis centres have a junior coaching scheme. Children can attend these lessons as complete beginners, but if they already know a little about the game from hitting with their parents they will have a valuable head start. Parents who coach their children should, however, be aware that bad habits picked up at an early age are difficult to break.

Tennis is by no means an easy game to learn. Initially, many children struggle just to hit the ball. However, they must be encouraged to persevere because once they have grasped the basics of hand-eye-ball coordination they will soon progress.

Opposite: Parents will need to encourage their kids to take tennis lessons when they first start playing.

45

PROGRESS TO COMPETITIVE TENNIS

COMPETITION WITHOUT THE PRESSURE

There is much debate about when children should begin playing competitive sport, and this controversy has inevitably pervaded tennis too. The most important thing is for youngsters to enjoy their tennis without undue pressure. Parents and coaches should let children progress at their own pace, providing support not stress and tension. There are many ways for children to learn and develop as tennis players – and supportive parents and coaches will help juniors to achieve success.

THE FUTURE OF TENNIS

Increasingly, in many tennis-playing countries, tennis authorities are recognizing that its future success depends on the development of a strong, vibrant mini game to attract young players into the sport and to retain their interest through to the full game. The approach varies between countries: the LTA in Britain and USPTA and PTR(US) in the United States have chosen a structured approach with clearly defined stages that enable players to develop an interest and progress to the full game.

In Britain, the LTA has relaunched Short Tennis and Transition Tennis as Mini Tennis. This is a three-stage system, and as children progress, the court size is bigger, the ball bounces faster, and the length of the game increases, making it easy to graduate to the full game. At each stage the children should always be able to play a game that they recognize as having all the features of the real game (www.minitennis.com). Little Tennis in the US aims to develop motor and tennis skills in children from the age of three upwards. In Australia, Tennis Australia have designed Fastennis for beginners of any age. Its different scoring system and quick format are designed to make the game attractive and easy to understand.

CHOOSING A COACH

When parents choose a tennis instructor for a junior, they should always select one with a qualification from the relevant national tennis association. In Britain LTA qualifications and a license are the ones to look for, while in the USA coaches should be registered to the USPTA and PTR(US). Independent coaches can be excellent too, but without official recognition from the governing body parents cannot be sure of the quality of teaching.

It is also important that the child gets on with his coach. A youngster who does not enjoy tennis lessons is unlikely to progress in the game. Individual lessons enable children to progress at a faster rate, but they are more expensive and not always as enjoyable as small group lessons, in which youngsters mix with their peers.

MAKE TENNIS FUN

Many parents make the mistake of taking their children's tennis too seriously. Nothing will stifle a child's natural enthusiasm more than a pushy parent. Youngsters should be encouraged not pressurized, and they should not have to go through hours of repetitive lessons and endless drills. Tennis matches and lessons should be enjoyable, so parents should try to find a coach with a sense of fun. Children should also be encouraged to pursue other sports too. Variety helps youngsters maintain their enthusiasm for tennis, as they feel refreshed when they play tennis after a break for another sport. In addition, the skills needed for other sports can help develop fitness and coordination, both vital for tennis.

In the past, many talented young professional players (generally girls) suffered from something called 'burn-out'. It is a problem caused by youngsters being pushed into playing so much tennis that their minds and bodies grow tired of the sport, forcing them to retire before they even reached their prime. Burn-out is unlikely to affect amateur players, but if adults don't make tennis a fun sport for children they will soon get bore and negative about the whole thing and direct their attention to another sport.

PLAYING TOURNAMENTS

Most tennis clubs have links with the junior competitive structure. Some clubs even have their own junior squads that travel as a group to tournaments. Different countries have different routes for juniors to follow if they want to play tournaments. The appropriate national tennis association will be able to provide any advice you need.

Parents, however, should realize that the junior tournament scene can be extremely competitive, and can involve a lot of travel and time away from home.

Early experience of tournament play can be useful for young players, but this advantage must be balanced against the stresses it puts on the youngster. Parents must be supportive of their children, whatever level they compete at, offering encouragement at all times. It should also be remembered that, just because a child struggles at junior tournaments, he may shine later on once fully developed.

TENNIS INJURIES

Tennis is a high-impact sport and some injuries may be inevitable, but many minor ones are avoidable.

STRAINS AND PULLS

The risk of getting minor injuries like this can be reduced dramatically by warming up properly before playing a game or doing drills. It need only take a few minutes, and is well worth the extra effort. After a game, it is advisable to put on a sweatshirt or jumper (and tracksuit pants if you are not changing into street clothes immediately) to allow your muscles to cool down slowly.

HANDS AND FEET

Badly fitting shoes and socks can contribute to blisters. The junior player should always get tennis shoes fitted properly. Ordinary trainers should not be worn for playing tennis. Blisters on the racket hand are probably the result of the racket grip being the wrong size for a player's hand. This is an easily remedied problem.

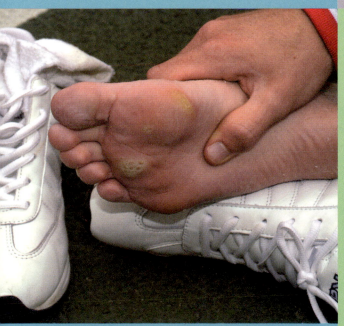

CRAMP

Cramp can occur either during or after playing, but the cause is the same: dehydration and loss of salts in the muscles. It most often affects the hamstrings and calf muscles. To prevent it, players should drink plenty, both before and during a match or practice session. If you feel thirsty, you are already dehydrated. A rehydrating sports drink will provide the salts that the muscles need.

DOS AND DON'TS

Do warm up properly and put on a warm top when you have finished playing

Don't stand around in sweaty clothes

Do wear well-fitting tennis shoes and socks

Don't play in normal trainers

Don't play if you are carrying an injury

Do go to your doctor

Do talk to your coach if you have a recurrent problem that may be related to a minor problem with your technique

Do drink plenty of water or a rehydrating (electrolytic) sports drink

Don't drink coffee, tea or soft drinks that contain caffeine

SPRAINED ANKLES

These are quite common because of the high impact nature of tennis. It is often very difficult to tell the difference between a bad sprain and a broken ankle, so any player with a bad ankle injury should go to the doctor or a hospital for a check-up. Avoid putting weight on the ankle until it is healed and do not attempt to play while it is painful.

LONGER-TERM INJURIES

Many tennis players suffer from long-term or recurrent injuries, affecting the back, knees, shoulder, elbow or wrist. Any long-term or recurrent problem should be seen by a doctor, and the player should not play unless told that he can. Such problems as tennis elbow and tendonitis in the wrists can take months to heal, or could even stop you playing completely.

Sometimes long-term injuries are simply the result of an accidental injury that fails to heal for one reason or another, but they may also be occur as a result of faulty technique. Any player who suspects that, for example, a recurrent back problem may be the result of a problem with his service action should discuss it with his coach.

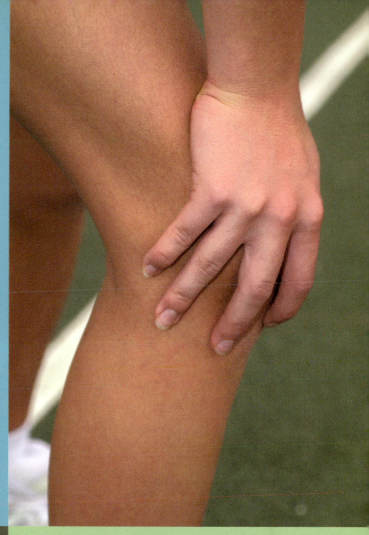

Some players do manage to carry on playing with knee injuries by wearing supports, but this is not advisable without medical advice, particularly for young players whose bones are still developing.

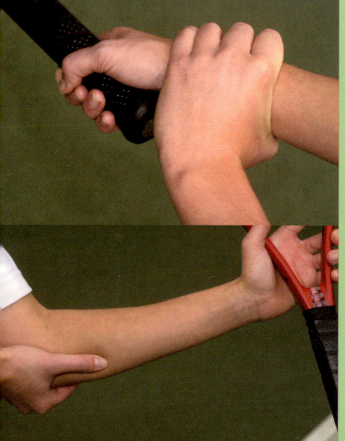

STARTING OUT

4

The aspiring junior tennis player needs just four things: a racket, a ball, a court and someone to hit with. Most towns have at least one public tennis court, so as long as it's not too wet and windy it is usually possible to play tennis without the need for an arduous journey. Inexpensive tennis rackets and balls are available from sports shops everywhere, and for players on a tight budget second-hand rackets can often be found in charity shops. As for someone to play with, because tennis is so popular there is always somebody among friends or family willing to hit with a junior player.

Opposite: Andre Agassi started playing tennis aged just four years old.

Left: Venus Williams has inspired many black kids around the world to take up tennis.

STRETCHING AND WARMING UP

To stay supple and avoid unnecessary injury it is crucial that players stretch their bodies, both before and after a match. Top players warm up for at least 20 minutes before they play, youngsters should stretch for at least ten minutes. In cold weather it is absolutely vital to warm up, as cold muscles are prone to injury. Junior players should make warming up part of their pre-match routine.

1 JOGGING AND BEFORE STRETCHING

Players should start with a five-minute jog around the court, this will raise the temperature of the muscles and prepare them for stretching. It will also increase the heart rate. Players should jog forwards, backwards and sideways, just as they will during the match.

Players must take care not to bounce their limbs as they stretch, as this can lead to pulled muscles. The body must be eased into each stretch, and the final position should be held for around ten seconds. Stretches should be repeated four or five times for each side of the body, alternating between left and right.

2 TRUNK ROTATION

The player stands with feet shoulder-width apart. He places his hands on his hips and twists all the way to the right. This position is held for ten seconds. The exercise is then repeated for the left-hand side.

3 QUADRICEPS

The quadriceps are the muscles on the front of the thigh. For this stretch the player must lean on a net post, or similarly stable object, for support. He grips his ankle and pulls it up towards his bottom, ensuring that his inner thigh and knees remain close together. The player must avoid leaning forward as he stretches. Do twice for each leg.

4 INNER THIGH

The player stands up with feet apart and toes pointing forwards, one leg straight and the opposite knee bent. He gradually places all his weight on the bent knee and eases his body down towards the floor. Feet must remain flat on the ground at all times. A net post can be used for extra support. Repeat on the other leg.

5 HAMSTRINGS

The hamstrings are the muscles at the back of the thigh, and if they are not warmed up properly it is easy to damage them. The player should sit on the ground, bend one leg to the side and stretch the other out in front of him, flat on the ground with toes and knee pointing upwards. As far as possible the back should be kept straight as he leans forward to touch his toes.

6 CALVES

The calf muscles are the ones at the back of the lower leg, and they are commonly affected by cramp and pulls. Players should stretch them by standing in a walking position with toes facing forwards, one leg back and straight and the other leg forward and bent. Slowly the body weight is transferred onto the forward leg, while the back heel is kept flat on the ground.

7 ARMS, ELBOWS AND WRISTS

The player's arms are positioned straight in front of his body with the palms facing upwards. With one hand, he stretches his wrist backwards and down (this position is held for ten seconds). He then stretches his wrist forwards and up towards himself (also held for ten seconds). Repeat four or five times and for both arms.

8 LUMBAR SPINE

The lumbar spine, which is the area in the lower back, comes under great strain when serving and smashing. Feet must be positioned apart and hands placed on hips. The player slowly bends backwards (not too far that he feels uncomfortable), keeping his knees straight and hips pushed forwards. The position is held for ten seconds and repeated several times.

9 TRICEPS

The triceps is the muscle underneath the upper arm. Players should stand, bend one arm up behind their head and with the opposite hand grasp their elbow, pulling it across and down until they feel the triceps muscle stretching. The non-racket arm must be stretched too.

10 PECTORALS

The pectoral muscles are the ones across the top of the chest, and they can be stretched by standing with one arm extended out to the side, holding onto the side netting or a net post. The player leans forward with his upper body until he feels the muscle stretch. Players should take care not to stretch too much, as they could damage their arm.

11 NECK MUSCLES

The player stands with feet apart, facing straight ahead. Gradually he bends his head down to one side, keeping his shoulders level. Repeat on the other side.

THE GRIPS

There are dozens of different grips in tennis, largely because there are dozens of different shots. Individual players use different grips for exactly the same shots, but it is a good idea for youngsters to learn the basic grips first. With confidence and improved technique, these grips can be adapted.

There are three basic grips that young players should learn: forehand (could be eastern or semi-western), the backhand (could be single- or double-handed) and the service or 'chopper' grip. The first two take their names from the USA, where the courts on the east coast used to be mainly made of grass and needed a grip that would allow the player to reach the low bouncing shots, while the courts on the west coast were mainly hard and needed a grip that enabled players to reach high-bouncing shots.

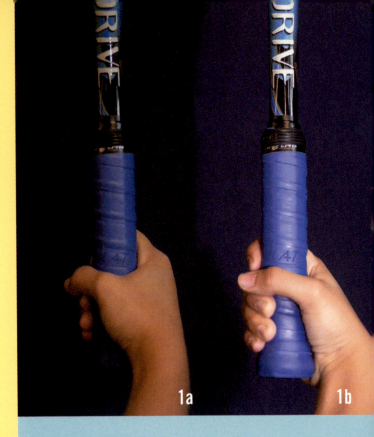

1a   1b

WHAT SIZE GRIP TO BUY?

New tennis rackets come in a variety of grip sizes. Players should try to buy rackets with the correct grip size for their hand (see page 20), but if they find it is too small they can build it up with an overgrip. Although not ideal, this solution prevents the player from having to buy a new racket. Some parents decide to buy a racket for their child with a grip size too large so that the youngster's hand can grow into it. Again, this isn't ideal, but the expense of buying new rackets can be a deciding factor. Don't forget that the wrong size grip will affect the player's shots and can cause tennis elbow.

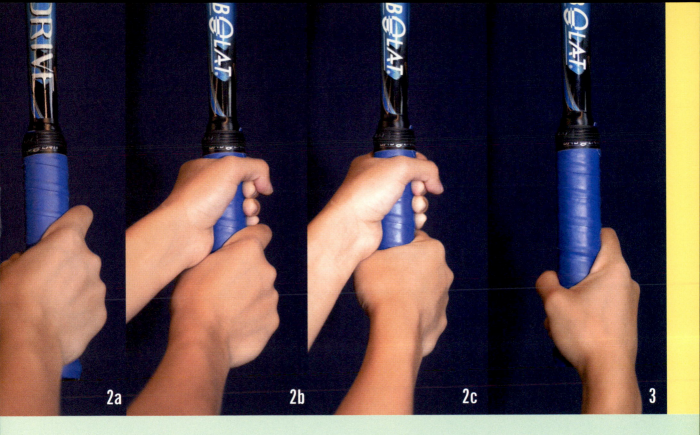

2a 2b 2c 3

1a THE EASTERN FOREHAND GRIP

The player should imagine that he is shaking hands with the racket. The 'V' shape between thumb and index finger must be lined up with the right-hand edge of the upper face of the racket handle as the racket head is held upright. This grip is perfect for flat or topspin forehands.

1b THE SEMI-WESTERN FOREHAND GRIP

To get to the semi-western grip the player should adopt the eastern grip and turn the handle of the racket in his hand slightly to the left. The 'V' shape between thumb and index finger should now be lined up with the left-hand edge of the right side face of the racket handle. This grip is used to hit high bouncing balls with topspin. Clay court specialists use a full western grip to create even more topspin. For this they turn the racket handle even farther round to the left.

2a THE BACKHAND GRIP

This is suitable for players who hit their backhands with just one hand. The racket handle is twisted to the right, so that the 'V' shape between thumb and index finger is lined up with the right-hand edge of the left face of the racket handle as you hold the racket head upright. Juniors who need extra control and power in their backhand may prefer a double-handed grip.

2b THE DOUBLE-HANDED BACKHAND GRIP (i)

The player places his right hand in the backhand grip position and puts his left hand directly above it in the eastern forehand position so that the hands are now touching each other. The player has less reach than with a single-handed backhand grip, but he will get more power in his shots.

2c THE DOUBLE-HANDED BACKHAND GRIP (ii)

The player places both hands in the eastern forehand grip position. This enables a flatter shot to be hit and involves less change between forehand and backhand grips. Players will also find it easier to disguise their shots.

3 THE SERVICE OR 'CHOPPER' GRIP

For this grip the player should imagine the racket is an axe or 'chopper'. The 'V' shape between thumb and index finger should be lined up with the left-hand edge of the upper face of the racket handle as you hold the racket head upright. Juniors will find it easier to start serving with an eastern forehand grip, but this can be changed to a chopper grip as they gain confidence.

THE KNOCK-UP

Once players have warmed up and stretched, it is customary to have a knock-up before the match begins. There are no hard and fast rules for knock-ups in junior tennis, but players tend to follow the lead of the professionals. In professional tennis, players have five minutes to warm up all their shots. They normally split this into three minutes to practise groundstrokes, volleys and smashes and two minutes to practise their serve.

GROUNDSTROKES

Players should start by exchanging forehands and backhands from the baseline. When suitably warmed up, one player should approach the net to practise volleys. Both players should try to keep rallies going by hitting volleys back to each other rather than away from each other, as they would in a match. Junior players should be reminded that during the knock-up it is more important to hits lots of strokes to get their eye in, rather than to play shots that an opponent cannot return. The full power winning shots should be saved for the match.

OVERHEAD SMASHES

After practising volleys, one player will usually indicate to his opponent that he wants to play some overhead smashes. One player feeds the other with easy lobs that can be smashed back to him. Players should not go for the kill with these smashes, instead they should use them to hone their eye for the match ahead. Each player must be given the chance to practise volleys and overheads. The idea of the knock-up is to have both players primed and ready for the real business of the match.

SERVE PRACTICE

The final two minutes should be kept clear for practising the serve. To avoid the risk of injury, it is a good idea if only players serve alternately. One player serves into the left-hand (deuce) court, then the other serves into the right-hand (advantage) court. Some players like to take the opportunity to practise their returns as well as their serves. This can be useful, because if a player goes into a match already having returned a few of his opponent's serves, he will be more used to it and so he is more likely to break his opponent early on in the match.

Once the knock-up has finished players should spin the racket, or toss a coin, to see who serves first and who plays at which end first (see page 32).

5

SERVE AND RETURN

The serve is the toughest stroke to learn in tennis, and because it is the only stroke that players have to play, it is also the most important. Many juniors find that they can play fairly good forehands, and average backhands and volleys, but when it comes to their serve they let themselves down. It is crucial that young players spend time working on their service technique.

When tennis first started in the 19th century, the service was supposed to be an equal and fair start to each rally. However, players soon began to perfect their service technique, thereby giving themselves a distinct advantage over the receiver. In modern professional tennis, the server's advantage is so strong that a competitive match might see just one or two games go against serve.

It is important to practise both serving and returning serve, and to learn to direct serves and returns to make it difficult for an opponent to get the ball back over the net to you. Drills can help players to hone their skills so that playing the best shots comes automatically.

Opposite: American Pete Sampras has one of the most consistently good serves in the world. With it he has won more Grand Slams than any other male player.

SERVE BASICS

The outcome of an entire match can often be decided by the relative strengths of the respective players' service games. Players with weak serves are unlikely to win a match, even if their other shots are strong. By contrast, players with strong serves can fare well, even if their other strokes are not so accomplished.

Because players have two chances to hit a good serve, they should aim to strike their first effort with both power and speed, while the second one should be hit slower and more carefully so as to guarantee that it lands in.

A FAILSAFE SECOND SERVE

When a player serves he has to stand behind the baseline and hit the ball at speed over a 0.91m (3ft) high net, into an area just 6m (21ft) by 4m (13ft 6in). At first this can be an extremely daunting task to the junior player, and even accomplished players find it difficult to combine both pace and accuracy. Players should also be reminded that everybody has days when they struggle to get their first serve in and when it seems like their whole serve has fallen apart. If this happens they should have a failsafe second serve which, while much slower, ensures that the ball goes in.

WHERE TO STAND

In singles, players serve from close to the centre mark, behind the baseline. This means they can cover the whole court when their opponent returns the ball, and they can also sprint to the centre of the net more quickly if they are playing serve and volley style tennis. Players must, however, take care to ensure that they stand the correct side of the centre mark; if they overstep the mark they will commit a foot fault. When serving into the left-hand service box, players should stand right of the centre mark, and if serving into the right-hand service box they must stand left of the mark. Players should never straddle the centre mark.

In doubles, the player serving should stand behind the baseline halfway between the centre mark and the inside edge of the sidelines. From this position, he will be able to cover the centre of the court if his opponent returns the ball there, but he will also be able to cover the sidelines too.

GRIP

For both the first and second serves, players should use the service or 'chopper' grip (see pages 56–7). Juniors will find it easier to start serving with an eastern forehand grip, but this can be changed to a chopper grip as they gain confidence.

QUICK TIPS

ACE

It is the ambition of every server to hit an ace. An ace is a serve that lands in the correct service box and is not touched by an opponent. It is really satisfying to hit an ace because the point is won outright and the opponent is left feeling helpless. Normally to achieve an ace, the player will have to strike the ball hard, fast, with perfect technique and out to one of the corners of the service box. It is rare to hit an ace on a second serve, because second serves are usually played with safety in mind and with less pace.

LETS

If the ball hits the net, or the net post, direct from a serve and lands in the correct service box, the players should play a let (i.e. play the serve again). Players are allowed as many lets as needed to complete the point. The ball must land in the correct service box to constitute a let.

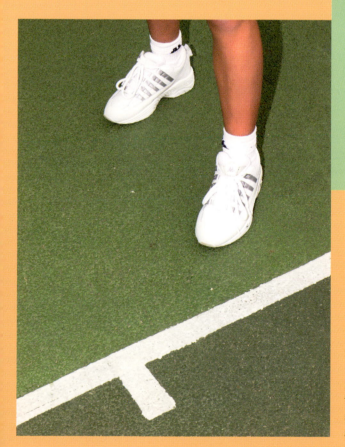

Opposite: Brazil's Gustavo Kuerten always enjoys excellent form on clay courts.

Left: Make sure your feet don't touch the baseline before you strike the serve because this will constitute a foot fault.

SERVING

Good serves have the following common elements to the throwing action

GRIP

The grip should be a chopper grip (see page 56-7), although when starting the player may find it easier to start with a forehand grip and gradually change it as he gets better.

STANCE AND POSITIONING

The starting position should be at a 45-degree angle to the baseline, with feet and legs shoulder width apart and with his weight on his front foot. He must prevent his feet from touching the baseline or the inside of the court before he strikes the ball, otherwise a foot fault will be called. Juniors often forget the foot-fault rule, so it is worth reminding them before they start playing competitive matches that players get penalized, but by then the habit can be difficult to break.

PREPARING TO SERVE

Before serving the player must decide where he wants to serve the ball and what type of serve it should be. Some players hold two balls in their non-serving hand but this is not advisable. However, players should always keep a second ball in their pocket or in a ball holder, so if they serve a fault they immediately have access to a ball for the second serve.

THE TOSS

The action's rhythm should be simple and smooth. The throwing action of the racket and ball placement should be one action. The ball placement arm should stretch up and release the ball at full stretch slightly in front and to the racket side of the body.

THE BACKSWING

As the ball is rising in the air, the player takes his arm back so that the racket head is extended away from the body into a throwing position with a bent elbow (see middle picture).

STRIKING THE BALL

Quickly but smoothly, the player whips his racket up over the top of his head to strike the ball above and slightly in front of himself, making contact at the point that the ball starts to fall back down towards the ground. His body and arm must be at full stretch when he strikes the ball to impart maximum height on the serve.

As the player strikes the ball, he should try to curl his wrist slightly downwards to avoid serving the ball long beyond his opponent's service box. (This curl of the wrist is called pronation.)

FOLLOW-THROUGH

The follow through should be on the non-racket side of the body and allow the player to move forwards slightly into the court and then to be ready for the next shot of the rally.

QUICK TIPS

TROUBLESHOOTING

If a player persistently serves into the net, the ball toss may be too low or too far in front of the player, so that the angle of the racket face is too closed.

If the ball is landing too long, beyond the end of an opponent's service box, the angle of the racket face may be too open, so a higher contact point, or a contact point farther in front may be needed.

BOUNCING THE BALL

Most players bounce the ball several times on the ground in front of them before they serve. Doing this aids concentration and helps them focus on the serve.

Most second serves are hit with more spin and less pace to ensure the serve goes in court.

SINGLES SITUATIONS: SERVING

The serve is a difficult but essential shot to master. There is no short cut. Players simply have to spend time practising their technique over and over again. A basket of balls and an empty court is a good way for a player to hone his service until it becomes second nature to him.

SERVE TARGETS

At first, junior players are happy just to get their serves over the net and in the correct service box. But as players progress and get better, they will want to start placing their serve in different parts of the service box. There are three places that players should aim at: the top left corner of the service box; the top right corner; and the top middle. The first two positions will force the receiver to move left or right, and the third position will go right into the receiver's body. The more a player practises placing his serve, the more lethal a weapon it will become.

WHERE TO SERVE TO

Once a junior player has sufficiently developed his serve, he will be able to choose whether to serve to the left, right or middle of the service box. If his opponent is weaker on the forehand, then he should serve to his forehand side, and if he is weaker on the backhand, he should serve to this side. If a player has a hard serve, he may want to serve at his opponent's body. This technique denies the opponent time and space to get his racket arm in the right position to return the shot.

Opposite: Martina Hingis does not have a powerful serve, but it is effective because of its accuracy and variation.

Left: Serving to an opponent's body is one of the most effective and useful shots a player can develop.

SERVE AND VOLLEY DRILLS

Although serving and volleying is an advanced tactic, players might want to try a number of serve and volley drills. Players should ask a coach or experienced player (if either are willing and available) to stand the other side of the net to them and return their serves. Immediately after the serve, the player should rush the net and play a volley. The senior partner should vary his returns – some high, some low, some down the middle and some out wide – so that the junior has to concentrate to make the volleys. Points are awarded for every successful volley. Care should also be taken to avoid foot faults when serving, as junior players will often make this mistake in their eagerness to get to the net quickly.

WHAT KIND OF SERVE

There are times when a player is unsure whether to hit a really hard serve or a safety serve. The right option will depend upon the match situation. If a player is 0-40 down and it is his second serve, then it would clearly be unwise to hit the ball too hard. However, if the player is 40-0 up, then he can afford to take a risk and go for an ace. It is common sense, but it is still worth pointing out to many junior players. Even if a player's service is not very strong, it is still a good idea for them to throw in the odd relatively fast, hard serve, just to keep their opponent on his toes.

TO SERVE AND VOLLEY OR TO STAY BACK

Another area where juniors face a dilemma, is whether to serve and volley or to stay behind the baseline after they have served. The answer will depend on the way they serve, their general style of play, how their opponent returns and what surface they are playing on. A player with a strong serve should consider playing serve and volley style, certainly after his first serve, unless of course he is playing on a very slow surface, for example clay, which will negate the power of his serve. If, however, a player has a weak serve and his opponent tends to return his serves very hard, then he should think about staying behind the baseline after serving. Both styles of play should be tried at the beginning of a match, and the most successful should be pursued.

QUICK TIPS

UNDERARM SERVE

Sometimes players find that no matter what they do, they cannot get their serves in. It happens to most players, and sometimes even affects the professionals. If all else fails, as a final resort, players may want to consider an underarm serve. Martina Hingis once adopted this approach when her overhead serves were not working in a match against Steffi Graf.

Players are not obliged by the rules to tell their opponent that they wish to switch to an underarm serve, although it would be rude if not to do so. The underarm should only be used in very exceptional circumstances, for example if the sun is right in a player's eyes or his toss up is affected by strong wind and his first serve just refuses to work.

The normal service or 'chopper' grip is used. The player must try to give the serve as much backspin as possible so that when the ball lands it bounces very low and short. This way his opponent will have to sprint forwards to reach the serve before it bounces twice. To give the ball backspin the server must open the face of the racket and slice under the ball.

WHEN SERVING GET THE BALL IN PLAY

This can be the hardest aspect of tennis for beginners but because it is the most important shot in the game, as it starts the game, it is vital to get the ball in play (drill 1, overleaf).

MOVE YOUR OPPONENT

As you progress you can learn first to make your opponent move by aiming to different part of the service box and then develop slice and topspin serves to help move the ball away from or into your opponent (drills 2 and 2a, overleaf).

KEEP A GOOD POSITION

Players should normally stand near the centre mark behind the baseline when serving in singles. But if a player thinks he can beat an opponent by serving out wide to the edge of the court, then he may want to move farther away from the centre mark to give himself more of an angle. Standing wide for the serve is risky, however, as it means that the opponent has more of the empty court to aim for on the return. Players must recover to the middle of the court quickly in this situation (drill 3, overleaf).

PLAY TO YOUR OPPONENT'S WEAKNESS

To do this you will need to be able to direct your serve so this is a similar practice to moving your opponent (drills 4 and 5, overleaf).

PLAY TO YOUR STRENGTHS

If you have a favourite serve, which works well for you and you feel confident about, then you need to recognize this and use that serve whenever possible (drills 4 and 5, overleaf).

PRACTICE DRILLS

DRILL 1
Players practise their serves starting from the service line. Every time they get a serve in, they move back one step towards the baseline.

DRILLS 2 and 2a
2 Serving to targets in the service box, the player has to nominate the target before each serve (see illustration opposite).
2a Serving to areas of the service box, the player nominates areas before serving. If he hits the area he wins the point, if he doesn't he loses the point.

DRILL 3
Practise serving, then recovering to the middle of the court in the ready position

DRILL 4
The server serves to the receiver's forehand who then returns to the server's backhand;, they then play the point competitively. If the initial pattern of two shots is not achieved then the point does not count (see illustration opposite).

   The drill is repeated with the server serving to the receiver's backhand and he then returns cross court.

DRILL 5
Players playing points, server loses the point if they do not play their favourite shot as their first groundstroke.

DRILL 2

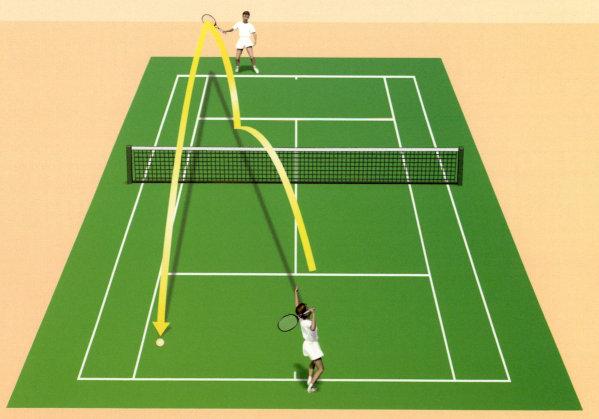

DRILL 4

1

2

THE SLICE AND TOPSPIN SERVE

Most second serves are hit with more spin and less pace to ensure the serve goes in court. Picture 1 shows the angle of the racket when hitting a flat first serve. Compare this with pictures 2 and 3 to see the different angles required for the slice and topspin serve.

THE SLICE SERVE

You may find it easier to begin with to place the ball slightly farther away from the racket side of the body. The ultimate goal will be to place the ball in the same place as the flat serve in order to disguise the type of serve.

3

SMALLER PLAYERS
Short players are at a distinct disadvantage when it comes to serving. Imagine that you could draw a line from where a player hits the ball on the serve to where it lands in his opponent's service box. For a very tall player this line would be straight, but for shorter players it would loop up and then down again. Very short players may have to jump in the air as they serve to get extra height. Look at the way Michael Chang serves. He is only 1.75m (5ft 9in) tall and has to use lots of topspin on his serve in order to get it in. Junior players can learn to hit their serves with topspin so that they loop the ball up, over the net and back down into the service box. To do this they need to brush the racket strings up and over the ball as they make contact. It is a tricky shot and players usually need coaching to perfect it.

STRIKING THE BALL
The racket will need to come around the outside of the ball with a slightly closed racket face in order to give the ball more slice. The follow-through will be on the non-racket side of the body (see picture 2).

THE TOPSPIN SERVE
The ball should be placed slightly farther back and over the head or non-racket arm. The racket head should be thrown up and across the ball. Imagine a clock face and the racket should move from 8 o'clock up and across to 2 o'clock. The player should remember to curl down the wrist to help control the serve (see picture 3).

SINGLES SITUATIONS: RETURNING

RETURN OF SERVE

To win a tennis match, players must break their opponent's serve, and to do this they will need to successfully return serve. The return of serve is a much-neglected aspect of the sport.

Youngsters will invariably be more concerned with individual strokes rather than the tactics of returning serve, but if you look at the professional game there are many players who have made the return of serve the most feared aspect of their game. Many smaller players on the tour, who perhaps don't have particularly strong serves, compensate for the games that they lose on their serve by breaking their opponent's serve. The way they do this is by having a killer return of serve.

WHERE TO STAND

It sounds obvious, but if an opponent has a very hard and fast serve then players should stand farther back than if he has a softer, weaker serve. As a general rule players should stand a little way behind the baseline when receiving, but not too far back or an opponent will be able to play a cheeky underarm or short serve or so far forward that they won't have enough reaction time to play a return. Players must also ensure they are covering both sides of their service box, so that they can reach a wide serve as well as one down the middle of the court.

READY POSITION

Players should never stand flat-footed as they prepare to return serve. They will be able to react much more quickly if they are on their toes and ready to move their feet. The racket should be held out in front, with the playing hand on the grip and the other hand supporting the throat of the racket if they have a single-handed backhand, or with both hands on the grip in the ready position if they have a double-handed backhand. The knees should be slightly bent, and the feet shoulder width apart. The receiver can now concentrate on the server.

WHAT KIND OF RETURN

If an opponent serves hard and fast, the only thing an opposing player can do is block the ball back to him. Instead of hitting right through a proper stroke, the player simply blocks the ball with his racket to slow it down and get it back over the net. A player will often get used to an opponent's hard serve during a match, gradually learning how best to return it, until eventually he is able to return the ball with pace, rather than simply

blocking it. Sometimes hard serves can be easier to return fast than softer ones, because it is simply a case of getting the racket to the ball and using the power of the serve. On soft serves, players must generate all the power themselves.

PERCENTAGE TENNIS

Many juniors think that the only way to win is to hit every ball as hard as they can, while praying that the shot goes in. This approach is rarely effective. In fact, an opponent will just wait for the inevitable mistakes. A much better approach is to play percentage tennis, whereby a player gives himself a greater chance of winning the point than his opponent. Instead of hitting the ball with maximum power, softer shots are placed

Above: prepare yourself for the return of serve by holding your racket out in front, your knees bent, your feet apart and your bodyweight on the balls of your feet.

Opposite: To receive a second serve you should stand slightly farther forward than you would to receive a first serve.

deliberately into particular areas of the court. A slow, sliced backhand into the far corner can be more effective than a super-fast flat forehand straight to an opponent. Brains win more points than brawn.

The first goal should be to make sure that all shots clear the net. Players should aim to clear it by at least 45cm (1ft 6in). If a player finds that his shots are going long, he will need to put more topspin on them so that they loop high over the net but still dip down quickly and land well within the baseline.

SERVICE RETURN DRILLS

It sounds obvious, but for every serve there has to be a return of serve. Most players practise their service technique like mad and forget to work on their returns. The answer is to develop a series of service return drills (see overleaf).

KEEP THE BALL IN PLAY

The easiest way of doing this is to aim the ball back towards the middle of the court (drills 1 and 1a).

MOVE THE OPPONENT

Once you can get the serve back then you need to try to move your opponent. Look at the court and see where the spaces are, this may very depending on where your opponent stands to serve (drills 2 and 4).

KEEP A GOOD COURT POSITION

When receiving you are standing to one side of the court so it is important that you regain a central position on the baseline after your return. Getting to this position will mean that you can cover the whole court for your opponent's next shot (drill 3).

PLAY TO YOUR OPPONENT'S WEAKNESS

On your return of serve it is a good idea to play to your opponent's weaker side. They will either not get the ball back or play a weaker shot that gives you the chance to win on the next shot (drills 2, 5 and 5a).

PLAY TO YOUR STRENGTH

If you have a stronger forehand then practise moving round your backhand to use your forehand, as long as you can still recover to a good court position (drills 5 and 5a).

PRACTICE DRILLS

DRILLS 1 and 1a

1 Players play points in the full court or cross court. If the receiver makes an error on the return, the server is rewarded with three points. This encourages the receiver to focus on consistency on the first shot of the rally.

1a Players work in pairs practising serve and return. The receiver scores 1 for a ball in play, 2 for past the service line and –1 for a miss. When the receiver gets to plus or minus 10, the players change roles, (see illustration opposite).

DRILL 2

One player serves, and the receiver must nominate where they are going to hit the return before the serve lands and then play the point out. This helps the receiver to focus on decision-making on the return of serve.

DRILL 3

Players practising in the singles court. The receiver practises his return, then recovers across the baseline ready to receive the next shot.

DRILL 4

The server gets a point for every serve that goes in, while the receiver gets a point for every return that goes to the server's backhand. When one of the players gets to 10 points, the players change roles.

DRILLS 5 and 5a

5 The server serves second serves to the receiver's backhand, and the receiver has to run around the ball to hit forehand shots alternately cross court and down the line.

5a The server serves second serves to the receiver's backhand and the receiver has to choose which ones to run around to play forehand.

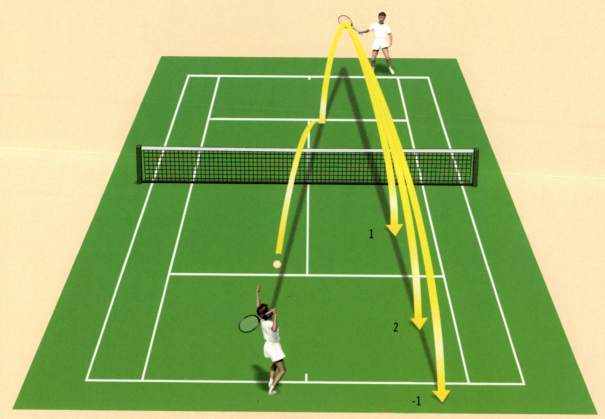

DRILL 1a

SINGLES SITUATIONS: BOTH PLAYERS BACK

Most points and games will be fought at the back for the court rather than at the net. It is therefore necessary for the player to understand how to construct points from this postion on the court.

ATTACK SHORT BALLS

Junior players frequently lack confidence, often choosing to play defensively and stay on the baseline, rarely approaching the net. This is 'chicken tennis'. If an opponent plays a short ball that lands near the service line, players should use the chance to attack the net. They should play the ball deep into a corner and approach the net to play the next shot as a volley. Very few youngsters will be able to beat an opponent at the net with a passing shot, especially if it is on their backhand side. Often, their only option when faced with an opponent at the net, is to put up a lob. Unless the lob is perfect, the player at the net should be able to get back, smash it and win the point.

Left: If a ball lands halfway up the court, use the opportunity to hit an attacking shot and then approach the net for a volley.

KEEP THE BALL IN PLAY

This is the area of play that is used most during a game, so it is very important that you can keep the ball in play once the rally has started (drill 1, overleaf).

MOVE YOUR OPPONENT

Look at the top players – they all do this so well. Once you can get the ball in you need to move your opponent to put them under pressure (drills 2 and 2a, overleaf).

KEEP A GOOD COURT POSITION

It is important to do this so that your opponent doesn't put you under too much pressure. Also remember that if you have hit a good shot not to stand and admire it as the ball may come back (drill 3, overleaf).

PLAY TO OPPONENT'S WEAKNESS

You need to find out your opponent's weaknesses and then exploit them (drill 4, overleaf).

USE YOUR STRENGTHS

You need to try to use your strengths as much as possible, especially to finish the point (drill 5, overleaf).

PRACTICE DRILLS

DRILL 1

Players work in pairs, with one thrower and one hitter. The thrower throws the ball anywhere in the service box to try to make the hitter move to the ball. The hitter has to control the ball back to the thrower. Every time the thrower catches three returned shots, the pair swap over.

DRILLS 2 and 2a

2 Both players start near the middle of the baseline, they then rally cross court, but have to try to return to the middle after each shot they hit.

2a Mark out an area in the centre of the court which the players should avoid. They play points or rally, but lose a point automatically if the ball goes in the marked out area. The marked out area grows as the player gets better (see illustration opposite).

DRILL 3

Set out two cones, one each side of the centre of the baseline. The players play points or rallies in the full court. The players have to recover back through the cones between each stroke (see illustration opposite).

DRILL 4

Players work in pairs, using a full court and play points One player plays in the backhand side of the court and can only play backhands, the other player has the full singles court.

DRILL 5

For once, the tramlines are in. Rallying cross court, both players are only allowed to hit forehands, even if they are rallying on the backhand diagonal.

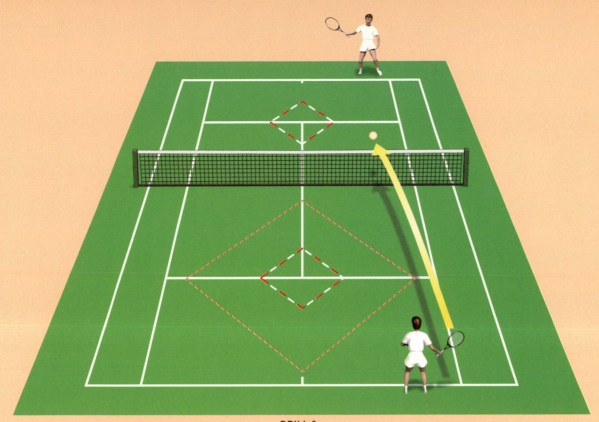

DRILL 2a

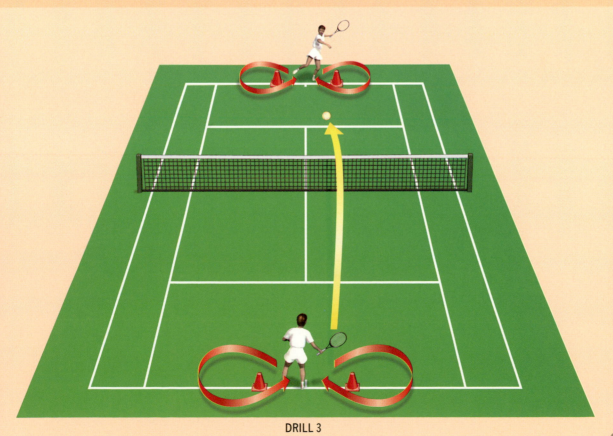

DRILL 3

THE FOREHAND

6

The forehand groundstroke is the first stroke a junior tennis player will learn, and it should be mastered as soon as possible so that basic rallies can be played. Forehands are probably the easiest shots to play and youngsters should make the fewest errors with them. The forehand will become the foundation and, hopefully, strong point of the junior's whole game.

There are three types of groundstroke on the forehand: flat, topspin and slice. The forehand slice is fairly rare and normally only used on faster, low-bouncing surfaces. Juniors are better off concentrating on the flat and topspin forehands, which are explained fully in the following pages.

Opposite: The forehand of Switzerland's Martina Hingis is one of the best in the women's game.

THE FOREHAND

All good basic forehands will have the following elements in common.

GRIP
For this shot players should use the semi-western or eastern forehand grip (see pages 56-7).

THE READY POSITION
Players must prepare for any shot by standing in the ready position. The player should be standing with the feet shoulder width apart, facing the net with knees slightly bent. Both hands should be on the racket, the player ready to react to the opponent's shot.

BACKSWING
Once the player realizes that the ball is coming to the forehand, the non-hitting hand should start the take-back and move together with the hitting arm so that the upper body rotates to a 90-degree angle to the net.

The non-racket arm should then act as a balance for the swing of the racket.

The footwork should allow the player to be balanced throughout the swing, so the last step should be towards the net.

STRIKING THE BALL
With eyes fixed on the ball as it moves and watching the ball onto the strings, the player should make contact with the ball to the side and slightly in front of the body at approximately waist height.

THE FOLLOW-THROUGH
The follow-through should be across the body in a low to high trajectory over to his left shoulder. The longer the follow-through, the more accurate the shot will be. The technique will alter slightly when hitting a flat or topspin forehand

TOPSPIN FOREHAND

Players could use a semi-western grip.

For a topspin forehand the player will take the racket back to a lower starting point and have the racket face slightly turned towards the ground. The face of the racket should still be slightly facing the ground at impact when the racket will brush up the back of the ball with a steeper low to high swing. This drags the strings up the back of the ball and makes the ball rotate forwards.

The player must follow up and over the ball to impart maximum spin.

FLAT FOREHAND

Players could use an eastern grip for this shot.

The swing will be a shallow low-to-high swing. When striking the ball the player will have their racket face 90 degrees to the ground.

FOREHAND VOLLEY

A volley is a shot hit from near the net before the ball bounces. It requires a sharp punching motion with a short follow-through and a firm grip. Never underestimate the importance of the volley. In doubles tennis, the team that controls the net with strong volleys is normally the winning team. In singles, especially on faster surfaces where the serve and volley style of play is dominant, the better volleyer will win if he can reach and control the net on a regular basis.

Many top professionals rush the net whenever their opponent gives them a short ball. A player is closer to his opponent when he plays a volley, so it is easier to play a winning shot.

From the net, players can strike a volley that is low off the ground, deep and at an angle. It is hard for an opponent to pick up a well-volleyed ball, and he will be under extra pressure because he has less time to react. If he is unable to hit a good passing shot, he will be forced to play the ball straight back to the volleyer at the net, which could set up a winning shot. His only alternative is to put up a lob, which can be smashed

The volley should be a short punch action. All good volleys should have common elements.

GRIP AND STANCE

Players should use the chopper grip (see page 56-7).

The ready position for the volley should be with the racket in front of the body, with the elbows up so that the player will move forwards to meet the incoming ball. The player should be positioned approximately 2m (6ft) from the net.

THE BACKSWING

The volley starts with the upper body turning to the racket side of the body. This will take the racket back far enough for a volley. Release the non-racket arm and move the racket forwards to contact the ball in front and to the racket side of the body. The upper body should lean towards the ball

STRIKING THE BALL

The front foot should go forwards the net and should make contact with the ground after the ball has been hit to balance the player. The player should punch at the ball with his racket head which should ideally be above the level of his elbow. The non-hitting arm should be used to balance the player and aid recovery.

FOLLOW-THROUGH

The follow-through should be very short and firm and allow the player to recover quickly.

THE SMASH

The smash is a power shot that is played by hitting the ball before it bounces, and while it is still high above the player's head. It is normally employed when an opponent mis-hits the ball and loops it up in the air, or in response to an intended lob.

Good players regard the smash as a free point. Provided the ball is not too far back into the court as it starts to fall, and the correct technique is used, even junior players should be able to put the ball away for a winner with ease.

Many players start to panic when an opponent puts up an easy lob, as they know they should kill the ball. Composure is essential, so if a player has any doubt about making the smash they should run back, let the ball bounce and play a normal groundstroke. They may not win the point with a killer shot, but they won't fluff it either.

STARTING POSITION

The correct starting position is essential for a good smash. Players should stand with feet apart, both legs must be slightly bent, the same distance from the net as for the volley.

GRIP AND STANCE

For the smash, players could use the 'chopper' grip (see pages 56-7). They must also adopt the ready position; standing with legs slightly apart, knees bent and head looking forward watching for the ball to come off their opponent's racket. As soon as a player realizes that his opponent has put a ball high above his head, and that the trajectory will enable him to hit a smash (rather than force him to run back for a lob), he must move quickly into position underneath where he thinks the ball will fall. Instead of running forwards or backwards into position, he should sidestep (with his body facing right) so that he is able to keep his balance. He should move to a position where the ball is above and slightly in front of the body.

THE BACKSWING

As the ball starts to drop, the player should point at it with his left hand. He should be sideways on, with the racket being taken back in a shortened service action. His eyes should remain focused on the falling ball at all times.

STRIKING THE BALL

As the ball drops closer to him, the player must quickly but smoothly throw the racket head up over the top of his head, striking the ball above and slightly in front of him. His body and arm should be at full stretch when he strikes the ball, the racket head should be thrown up at the ball to strike it at maximum height.

THE FOLLOW-THROUGH

Players should follow right through the smash in the direction of the ball, bringing the racket back down and to the left-hand side of the body.

The follow-through should allow the player to recover for the next shot. If an opponent manages to get a racket to a smash, his return is likely to be another high, looping ball which will require a second smash.

QUICK TIP

SMASHING AFTER A BOUNCE

Occasionally, one player puts the ball so high up into the air that it is possible to play a smash even after the ball has bounced. This is easier to do because the bouncing ball will not be travelling so fast when it is struck. The same technique is used, but players must get into position quickly after the ball bounces.

DROPSHOT

The dropshot is played by nudging the ball over the net so that it bounces short, giving an opponent no chance to reach it before the second bounce. A player should only employ a dropshot if his opponent is far back, behind or at the baseline and will be unable to reach the ball in time. Also, by putting backspin on the shot the ball will bounce very low and very short.

It is a very delicate shot to make, and players must deaden the pace of the ball to send it soft and low over the net. Dropshots are most effective on soft courts such as clay or grass, where a softly played ball will not bounce high. On high-bouncing hard courts an opponent has more time to reach the ball before its second bounce. The dropshot will usually be played off a shorter ball that the player could also attack.

GRIP AND BACKSWING

For both the forehand and backhand dropshot, players could use the 'chopper' grip (see pages 56-7). Players should adopt the ready position as they watch for the ball to come off their opponent's racket. As soon as a player decides that he wants to play a dropshot, he should place his non-racket arm, slightly bent, out to the front on his left-hand side to provide balance. At the same time, he should start taking the racket back behind the right-hand side of his body.

STRIKING THE BALL

The player must now turn his body round to the right and start moving towards where the ball will land. Keeping his eyes fixed on the ball as it moves in his direction, he must step towards it and swing the racket head towards it. He should bend his knees a bit more than he would for a normal forehand groundstroke; this will help to keep the ball as low as possible. Ideally, the ball should barely clear the net.

He should connect with the ball to the side and slightly to the front of his body. The hitting arm should be slightly bent and the non-racket arm used to help balance the player. The face of the racket must be open (i.e. almost facing the sky) and the racket should be swung right under the ball so that when the player connects, his racket slices underneath it in a chopping action, thereby imparting plenty of backspin.

FOLLOW-THROUGH

A shorter than normal follow-through is required with a dropshot. The speed is taken off the ball by reducing the length of the forward swing. However, players should not be too cautious, because if the follow-through is too short the shot will have insufficient backspin.

QUICK TIPS

CARESS THE BALL

Instead of using a punching motion, like on a volley, or a full swinging motion, as on a groundstroke, for the dropshot players should caress the ball over the net. The racket should be brought right under the ball in a slicing motion and, using the wrists, the ball should be guided softly over the net.

EXTREME BACKSPIN

After much practice on the dropshot, players will be able to put so much backspin on the ball that when it lands it will bounce directly upwards rather than forwards in the direction struck. Some players can even make the ball bounce back in the direction it is hit from. A perfect dropshot is one that lands softly, bounces low and has so much backspin on it that the ball spins back towards the net.

FOREHAND LOB

Players must remember they are playing a shot that has to go very high over the net. The basic swing to the forehand or backhand will need to be exaggerated with a bigger low to high swing. Lobs are most effective against shorter players, as it is easier for players to maintain control of the shot as they play the ball over a shorter opponent's head and beyond the reach of his racket. Against taller players lobs are very difficult, because if the ball is not high enough they will smash it. Players are forced to loop the ball really high over the heads of taller opponents, which inevitably gives the opponent time to run back and play the ball after it has bounced.

The best option is the topspin lob. This shot makes it possible for players to hit the ball fairly hard, because the spin prevents it from landing outside the back of the court. Also, balls with topspin bounce both quickly and farther, so if an opponent tries to chase the ball he will find it bouncing away from him and out of reach.

GRIP AND BACKSWING

For the forehand lob, players could adopt the semi-western grip (see pages 56-7) and the ready position as they watch for the ball to come off their opponent's racket. As soon as a player realizes that the ball is coming to his forehand side, he should place his non-racket arm, slightly bent, out to the front on his left-hand side to aid balance. At the same time, he should start taking the racket back behind the right-hand side of his body, fairly low to the ground.

STRIKING THE BALL

The player must now turn his body round to the right and start moving towards where the ball will land. Keeping his eyes fixed on the ball as it moves in his direction, he steps towards the ball with his left foot and swings the racket head up towards it. He should connect with the ball to the side and slightly to the front of his body. The hitting arm should be slightly bent. Because he is aiming to lob the ball the swing

must come more low to high. He must keep the racket head level, his eyes should remain on the ball at all times, following it as it connects with the racket strings.

THE FOLLOW-THROUGH

The player should follow up and over the ball as he hits it to give it maximum topspin. He then brings his racket up and across his body, over to the area above his left shoulder. The longer the follow-through, the more topspin on the shot. The more topspin, the farther the ball will bounce, and the harder it will be for an opponent to chase it down. The player must now return to the ready position, just in case he hasn't given the shot enough height and his opponent is able to smash the ball back.

QUICK TIP

LOB TO THE BACKHAND
Players should be encouraged to lob to their opponent's backhand side. That way, even if the lob is too low, he will be forced to play a backhand smash rather than a forehand one. Backhand smashes are the most difficult shots to play in tennis, and an opponent is far more likely to fluff it.

THE BACKHAND

The backhand is a shot struck on the left-hand side of the body, in the case of a right-handed player, or the right-hand side for left-handers. The vast majority of youngsters are weaker on the backhand side than on the forehand side, this is because they find it a less natural movement. Opponents will try to exploit this weakness by putting pressure on the backhand, so it is essential that players practise their backhand until they are totally confident with it. Players should aim be equally strong on both sides however, most players do have a stronger side which they favour. Young players should be discouraged from running around a backhand ball to play it with a forehand shot, as this is no long-term solution. Sooner or later players will have to use their backhand, so it is better to work on it at a young age.

There are three types of groundstroke on the backhand: flat, topspin and slice. The flat and topspin backhands can be played with either a single- or double-handed grip. Players using a double-handed backhand will find it easier to hit a sliced backhand single-handed. Most younger players will find it easier to play double-handed on this side.

Opposite: Russia's Yevgeny Kafelnikov loves to hit the ball immediately after the bounce.

95

THE BACKHAND

Good backhands have the following common elements to them.

THE GRIP
Players could use the single-handed backhand grip (see pages 56-7).

THE BACKSWING
When the player realizes the ball is coming to his backhand side the shoulders should be turned and the non-hitting hand used on the racket take-back, which should be below the height of the ball.

STRIKING THE BALL
The movement pattern and footwork should allow the player to maintain balance and the last step should be towards the net. At the same time the player should be swinging the racket towards the ball. The contact point should be to the side and in front of the body.

FOLLOW-THROUGH

The racket should follow through to a high point across the body in the direction where the ball is aimed.

TOPSPIN BACKHAND

For a topspin backhand the player will take their racket back to a lower starting point and have their racket face slightly turned towards the ground. The face of the racket should be slightly closed to the ground at impact when the racket will brush up the back of the ball with a steeper low-to-high swing. This drags the strings up the back of the ball and thus makes the ball rotate forwards.

The player must follow up and over the ball to impart maximum spin.

SLICE AND DOUBLE-HANDED BACKHAND

All players need a slice backhand. Players with a double-handed backhand will need to develop a single-handed slice backhand to use under pressure.

THE GRIP

For the single-handed slice backhand, players could use the backhand, chopper or slightly eastern forehand grip (see pages 56-7).

THE BACKSWING

The shoulder turn should be helped by the use of the non-hitting hand to take the racket back to a point above the height on the incoming ball. The movement pattern and footwork should allow the player to maintain balance and the last step should be towards the net.

STRIKING THE BALL

While the player is stepping towards the ball the swing should slice under the ball and then follow the path of the ball. The contact point should be to the side and in front of the body with the racket face open at 45 degrees. The non-hitting arm should be used to balance the player.

FOLLOW-THROUGH

The player brings his racket forward and down, extending the arm out, in front of the body.

DOUBLE-HANDED BACKHAND

Players could use the double-handed grip (see page 56-7). The basic technique is the same as the single-handed shot, but the shoulder turn rather than the non-racket hand that drives the racket take-back.

The contact point should still be to the side and in front of the body and the racket should follow through to a high point across the body.

BACKHAND VOLLEY

THE GRIP AND STANCE

For the backhand volley players could again use the chopper grip (see page 56-7). The player should be in the ready position with the racket in front of the body, elbows up ready to move forward to meet the incoming ball.

THE BACKSWING

The shoulders should be turned, using the non-hitting hand to keep the racket head firm. This degree of shoulder turn will take the racket back far enough for the volley.

STRIKING THE BALL

The contact point should be in front and to the side of the body and the front foot should go towards the net, the player's momentum should be going forward. The non-hitting arm should be used to balance the player and aim recovery.

THE FOLLOW-THROUGH

This should be very short and firm and allow the player to recover quickly. The player must return to the ready position as soon as the shot is played just in case he has to play another volley.

BACKHAND LOB

The backhand lob should be played almost identically to the forehand lob, except on the left-hand side of the body, rather than the right-hand side.

GRIP AND STANCE

For the backhand lob players should use the single- or double-handed backhand grip (see pages 56–7). When the player realizes that the ball is coming to his backhand side, he should twist his shoulders round to the left, taking the racket back behind his body (fairly low to the ground) with his left hand on the throat of the racket, if using a single-handed grip. The player should now start moving his right foot forward, towards where the ball will land, releasing his left hand from the throat of the racket.

BACKSWING

Keeping his eyes fixed on the ball as it moves in his direction, the player must step towards the ball with his right foot, simultaneously swinging the racket head towards it.

STRIKE THE BALL

The player should connect with the ball to the side and slightly to the front of his body. His hitting arm should be slightly bent and the face of the racket should be pointing slightly upwards. The racket head must remain at this angle.

FOLLOW-THROUGH

The player must follow up and over the ball to impart maximum topspin. The racket is then brought up and across the body over to the area above the player's right shoulder. The longer the follow-through, the more topspin on the shot, and the more topspin on the shot the farther it will bounce, and the harder it will be for an opponent to chase it down.

Above: Greg Rusedski (left) and Tim Henman (right) are the top two players in Britain and have inspired countless British youngsters to play.

DOUBLES

Doubles tennis is both rewarding and challenging, requiring a different set of tactics and skills to the basic singles game. That said, many players find it thoroughly enjoyable and that the different techniques learned actually improve their singles game.

Doubles can be much faster than singles, and reaction times are speeded up: you will often see more reflex shots in doubles tennis. Play at the net is an important aspect of this form of tennis, and passing shots need to be even more accurately placed, simply because there are two people waiting on the other side of the net rather than one.

Doubles tennis is about cooperating with and supporting your partner. Each of you will bring strengths and weaknesses to a partnership, and good doubles play is about combining your skills to make a team that is stronger than the sum of its parts.

DOUBLES TACTICS

WHICH SIDE TO PLAY ON

Players should get used to playing on the same side every time they play doubles. In a partnership that plays together regularly, one person should always play on the right and one should always play on the left. As a basic rule, right-handed players with stronger backhands should play on the left, while right-handers with stronger forehands should play on the right. If one player is a right-handed player and one a left-handed player, it makes sense to put the 'leftie' on the left where he can play wide shots on the forehand, and the 'rightie' on the right where he can also play wide shots on the forehand.

Sometimes it's a good idea to put the stronger player on the left so that his greater skill and experience will help win crucial points, such as when you are 40–0 down, 40–30 down or when the opposing team has the advantage point. However, there is no rigid rule for who should play on which side in doubles. Players should be encouraged to go with the solution that works best and they should not be afraid to experiment.

CONTROL THE NET

The winning team in doubles is almost always the one that best controls the net. It is very hard to hit winners from the baseline, because there are two opponents covering the other side of the court, but from a net position it is possible to angle volleys out wide, or down the middle between the two opponents.

Both players should aim to get to the net as quickly as possible. The team that reaches the net first will dominate rallies and, provided their volleying is sound, create a wall that the other team cannot breach.

Faced with a team at the net, opponents have two options:
1 Hit the ball hard at the opposing players (a tactic that is not difficult to deal with, providing both players react quickly to the volley).
2 Lob both players (also unlikely to be successful, as one player will probably get back to return the ball).

Players should be reminded to keep volleys low and deep near the opposite baseline. By doing this, opponents will have to scoop up the ball, giving an easy next volley that should be put away for a winner.

Opposite: The 'Woodies' (Australian players Mark Woodforde (left) and Todd Woodbridge (right)) were two of the best doubles players ever.

COMMUNICATION

There may only be two players in a doubles partnership but it is still a team, so it is vital that both players communicate with one another. It is not necessary for doubles partners to be best friends off the court, but when playing a match, each player should know exactly what the other is thinking at all times on the court.

The Australian team known as 'the Woodies' (Todd Woodbridge and Mark Woodforde) were among the world's most celebrated doubles teams, and their success owes much to their excellent communication. They speak to each other between points, encouraging one another with high fives and slaps on the back. Junior doubles players can learn from their example.

As the match wears on, doubles players should analyse the game and discuss with their partners what is working and what is not. The net player can help the server by suggesting different ways of serving, and the server can help the net player by suggesting volley alternatives. Whatever happens, if one player starts making bad mistakes, his partner should not criticize him. He should keep encouraging him and congratulate him on every good shot.

Players must also call for the ball as soon as possible in doubles. If there is any ambiguity over who should play a shot, the player who shouts 'mine' first should always take it. Both players will look very silly if they assume that their partner is going to play the ball and it bounces between the two of them. Likewise, if both assume that the ball is theirs without calling for it, and they collide while trying to play it, they will not only look silly but also end up with some nasty bruises.

Opposite: Sisters Serena and Venus Williams often play as a doubles team.

Opposite below: Always encourage each other between points.

Below: Hand signals are a great way to tell your partner which direction to serve.

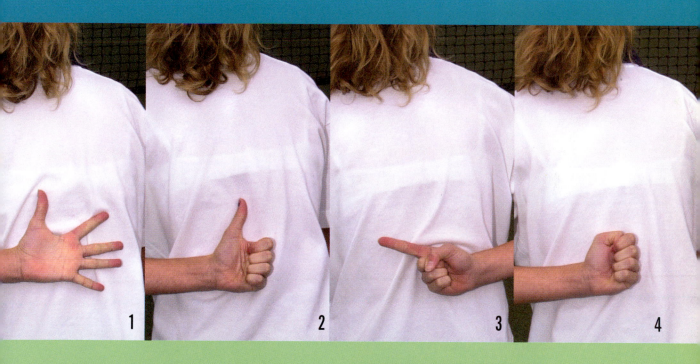

1   2   3   4

HAND SIGNALS

Many doubles teams use signs to communicate secretly with one another. The player at the net will make the sign with his hand behind his back so that only his serving partner can see it. Ideally each hand signal should have two parts to it. The first sign will tell the server where to serve to (out wide, down the middle or at the receiver's body), while the second will indicate whether the net player plans to intercept

WIDELY USED DOUBLES HAND SIGNALS.
1 spread hand – I'm going to intercept
2 thumbs-up sign – serve down the middle
3 finger pointed sideways – serve out wide
4 clenched fist – I'm going to stay on my side

across on the return or stay on his side of the court.

The signals can be anything, as long as they are clearly seen and both players understand them.

POSITIONS FOR DOUBLES

In doubles, where players stand on the court is just as important as the way they hit the ball. Remember that two players are covering an area over 130sq m (more than 1,400sq ft), so if they are not in the right position their opponents will easily be able to put the ball beyond their reach. Ideally, both players should aim to get to the net as quickly as possible, from where the rally can be ended with a volley. But where should players stand at the beginning of a point?

ONE UP, ONE BACK

This is the traditional doubles formation. The server should stand behind the baseline about halfway between the centre mark and the farthest tramline. From here, if he is a serve and volleyer, he can run directly to a central volley position after serving, or if he is a baseliner he can cover a return down the middle or out wide in the sidelines.

The server's partner should be at a net position. He should be standing in the service box, halfway between the line dividing the two service boxes (the centre line) and the nearest sideline. He should not be too close to the net or he won't have time to react for a volley. About halfway between the net and the service line is ideal.

The service returner should stand in a return of service position: just behind the baseline, in a central position from where he can cover serves out wide and down the middle.

The returner's partner should stand on the service line, halfway between the centre line and the nearest sideline. From here he can move forward to play a volley, but he can also get back for a lob over his head.

'I' FORMATION

For this formation, the server stands very close to the centre mark in the middle of the baseline, and the server's partner squats down in the middle of the court, a couple of steps forward from the service line. From here he can intercept the return either on the left or the right. He has to squat down in order to avoid being hit by the serve.

Before they start the point, the players agree who is going to move and cover which side of the court. The net player can use finger pointing signs behind his back to indicate secretly which way he is going to cross. The server should then cover the opposite half of the court. Both players must be sure who is going to which side, and they must agree who will take balls down the middle.

The good thing about the 'I' formation is that it often flusters the service returner. All the movement can put him off, so it is a great tactic for a doubles team that is being punished by really hard service returns. The serve is aimed down the middle, towards the 'T' so that the service returner is unable to play the ball down the line beyond the reach of the server. Unless a player has a very strong second serve, doubles teams should only really use the 'I' formation on a first serve.

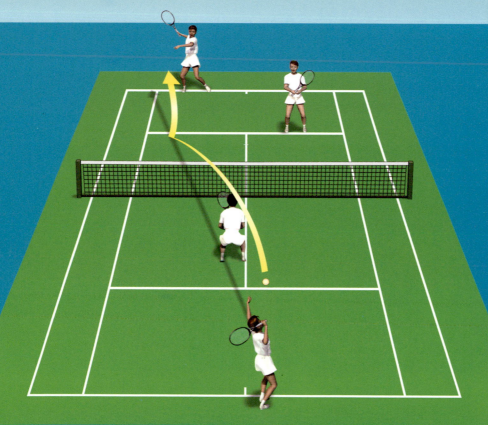

AUSTRALIAN FORMATION

If players find that their serves are being punished with hard cross court returns, they may want to try the very unusual Australian formation. The server's partner stands at the net on the same side of the court as the server, in order to volley any cross court returns. The server then has to cover any returns down the line. This position will look very strange, because at the start of the point both players are on the same side of the court.

Like the 'I' formation, the Australian formation works best with hard, fast serves, so it should only be used on first serves. The server will find it hard to run across for a wide return down the tramlines, so he should try to serve down the middle and force the receiver to return back into the middle of the court.

QUICK TIP

PICK ON ONE PLAYER
In both doubles and mixed doubles, players find it is very tempting to pick on the weaker player on the opposing team by consistently playing all the shots to him. In competitive tennis this is totally acceptable and common practice, but if a player does it in social tennis he may well be considered rude and unsportsmanlike.

BOTH BACK FORMATION

If players find that they are losing points when standing at the net, as a really defensive move they can adopt the 'both back formation'. This is risky, because it allows the opposing team to dominate the net, but it does provide more time to react to shots. It will also provide more opportunity to hit effective lobs over the heads of opponents. If this formation is adopted, players should still both aim to get to the net when the situation allows; if they do not, they are unlikely to win because it is difficult to get sufficient points from the baseline. Both players can start on the baseline, but ideally they should both eventually get to the net to finish off the point with volleys.

OFF-COURT PRACTICE

Not everyone has access to an indoor tennis court. During the winter, when the evenings close in and the weather gets worse, players are often unable to get on court, however, there are many tennis activities that can be used to maintain interest throughout the colder months. Players should, of course be warned to take care not to break any ornaments!

Opposite: If you haven't got an opponent to play with, you can always practise against a wall.

GAMES TO PLAY AT HOME

1 BOUNCE THE BALL

So as to keep their hand-eye coordination up to scratch, players should try bouncing a tennis ball on the side of the frame of their racket head. It takes quite a lot of practice, but eventually they will be able to walk around the room as they do it.

2 WALL VOLLEYS

If players have a flat wall in their garage or garden, they can practise volleys against it. They should try to use the correct volley grip, and remember to bend their knees just as they would on court. As players get better they can move closer to the wall, thereby giving themselves less reaction time.

1

3 HOT POTATO

This exercise requires at least three players. The players stand in a line, with a racket each. The objective is to try to get the ball, as quickly as possible, from one end of the line to the other by passing it from racket to racket without touching any hands along the way.

4 STORK

Balance is critical to tennis players, and juniors can improve theirs by practising what is called the 'stork position'. The player stands on one leg, with arms outstretched and eyes closed, maintaining balance. As he wobbles around, he must try to remain standing. This exercise will also strengthen the player's ankles.

7 VIDEOS AND VIDEO AND COMPUTER GAMES

Junior players should not be allowed to turn into couch potatoes during the winter, but coaches and parents should not underestimate the value of watching tennis videos and playing tennis video and computer games. There are many coaching videos on the market, most of which show experts playing shots the correct way. Even watching professional tennis matches will provide valuable hints on technique and tactics. Tennis video and computer games are useful too. Games won't help with technique and stroke play, but they will help hand-eye coordination.

5 GRIP STRENGTHENING

When tennis balls get old and worn they start to go soft. Players should not throw them all out, because squidgy balls can be used to strengthen racket grip. Players squeeze the ball with their hand for five seconds and then repeat 30 times. The non-playing grip must be practised as well, otherwise the player will end up with one hand stronger than the other.

6 EGG AND SPOON

The player walks around the house holding his racket with a ball balanced on the strings. As he gets better, he can try walking over obstacles or up and down stairs. To make it even more difficult he can place more balls on his racket strings.

8 SERVICE ACTION PRACTICE

To develop and improve the service action the players can spend time throwing practice rugby balls* or 'vortex' balls to each other. As the players get more proficient they can stand farther apart and vary the tradjectory of the ball. These balls can be bought from sports and toy shops.

*these balls are small, similar in size to practice footballs.

9 UPPER BODY ROTATION

This drill will help coordination and improve the rotation of the upper body from the hips when hitting either forehand or backhands shots.

   Take a medicine ball or football, ensuring it is not too heavy, and stand roughly 1.5m (5 ft) away from your partner. The players then throw forehands to each other. Then reverse the drill and throw backhands. If the players have double-handed backhands, practise thowing backhands with an open stance. This will impove your coordination and timing on the shot.

10 FOOTWORK PATTERS

This will improve your footwork and change of pace. Set up a number of short cones about 0.3m (1ft) apart. The distance between the last two cones should be approximately 1.5m (5 ft). Players run between the cones (one step between the cones) and then sprint the distance between the last two cones. The number of cones and the distance between the last two cones can vary with practice and to keep you interested in the drill.

   A good variation of this drill is for players stand sideways on and run through the cones in a figure of eight pattern. Players use small foot movements going forwards, sideways, backwards and then sideways again to get to the end of the row of cones.

9a

9b

10a

10b

11

12

13a

13b

13c

11 FIGURE OF EIGHT THROWING

The players start by standing facing each other about 3m (10ft) apart, holding one ball in either hand. In one continuous motion the players throw the balls in their right hands, while at the same time passing the ball from their left hand to the right before catching the ball just thrown by their partner in their left hand. This will take some time to get used to, but once conquered it will help improve hand-eye coordination. The number of balls used can be increased when players get more proficient. Players can also move sideways while carrying out this drill for further coordination with the feet.

12 ONE BOUNCE SPRINT

This drill aims to improve reaction time and sprinting from a stationary position. The players stand about 2m (7ft 9in) apart: again this distance can change with practice. One player holds his arms out the the side, each hand holds a ball, plams facing down. The player then drops one of the two balls he is holding. The second player must catch the ball after one bounce. The farther away the players are, the quicker the sprinting player has to be.

13 THE OVER AND UNDER

This again tests reaction time and speed of the players. One player stands behind the other with a ball. The player with the ball throws the ball either in the air or along the ground in front of the second player. The second player has to retrieve the ball before it reaches a pre-determined point.

QUIZ

This special tennis quiz will test the junior player's knowledge of the sport. All the answers can be found within the pages of this book. Youngsters should do the quiz with tennis-playing friends or family members. See who knows most about tennis in your family.

FIRST SET

1 When was modern tennis invented?

a The 1780s

b The 1850s

c The 1920s

d Last summer

2 In which country was modern tennis first played?

a Great Britain

b USA

c Australia

d Azerbaijan

3 Which of the following tournaments is not a Grand Slam event?

a Wimbledon

b US Open

c Spanish Open

d Australian Open

4 What does ATP stand for?

a Association of Tennis Professionals

b American Tennis Partnership

c Affiliation of Tennis Players

d Awfully Terrible Players

5 What does WTA stand for?

a Western Tennis Affiliation

b Women's Tennis Association

c Worker's Tennis Area

d Wicked Tennis Artists

6 What is the name of the tournament venue for the US Open?

a Los Angeles Tennis Centre

b Flushing Meadows

c Wimbledon

d Disneyland

SECOND SET

7 What is the name of the women's international team tournament?

a WTA Cup

b Women's World Cup

c Fed Cup

d Butter Cup

8 What is the name of the plastic strip along the top of a racket head that prevents it from getting damaged?

a Top strip

b Protection strip

c Bumper strip

d Strip tease

9 What is special about indoor tennis shoes?

a They have completely smooth soles

b They haven't been invented yet

c They have no laces

d They are illegal

10 How long is a tennis court?

a 15.24m (50ft)

b 23.77m (78ft)

c 26.2m (86ft)

d 6.4km (4 miles)

11 How high should the net be in the middle?

a 0.914m (3ft)

b 2.13m (5ft)

c 1.52m (7ft)

d As high as a house

12 What is the name of the line that divides the two service boxes?

a Baseline

b Service line

c Centre line

d Line dancing

THIRD SET

13 The first player to get how many points wins a tiebreak?

a Three

b Five

c Seven

d Four hundred

14 How old was Pete Sampras when he started playing tennis?

a Three

b Five

c Seven

d Twenty-eight

15 What is a more common name for lateral epicondylar tendonitis?

a Tennis elbow

b Tennis arm

c Inflamed elbow

d Chicken pox

16 Which of the following is NOT a recognized tennis grip?

a Eastern grip

b Semi-western grip

c Northern grip

d Western grip

17 Approximately how long should you play the knock-up for?

a Four minutes

b Five minutes

c Ten minutes

d Four hours

18 Which of the following is NOT a type of spin in tennis?

a Gyrospin

b Topspin

c Slice

d Backspin

FOURTH SET

19 What should you do after playing an approach shot?

a Stay behind the baseline

b Replay the point

c Rush to the net

d Give up and go home

20 What kind of follow-through should you use on a volley?

a A long, swinging one

b A short, sharp punching motion

c Through your legs

d Let go of the racket and watch it follow the ball

21 What should you do with your non-playing hand when you hit a smash?

a Wave at your opponent

b Point at the ball

c Hold the throat of the racket

d Paint your fingernails

22 What is NOT a good option if your opponent is at the net?

a Lob him

b Play a passing shot

c Play the ball hard at him

d Dropshot

23 What is the main disadvantage of using a double-handed backhand?

a You have less reach

b You have less power

c A double-handed backhand is a foul shot

d You won't be able to wave at your opponent

24 Which is the trickiest shot to play in tennis?

a Forehand volley

b Backhand slice

c Backhand smash

d A lob

FINAL SET

25 What is the best way to move into position for a smash?

a Huge strides

b Lots of short side steps

c Skipping

d Handstands

26 What is the term used for when your foot touches the baseline before you serve?

a Foot fault

b Service fault

c Double fault

d Foot in mouth

27 What is the name of the short line halfway along the baseline?

a Service mark

b Foot mark

c Centre mark

d Deutschmark

1 b The 1850s

2 a Great Britain

3 c Spanish Open

4 a Association of Tennis Professionals

5 b Women's Tennis Association

6 b Flushing Meadows

7 c Fed Cup

8 c Bumper strip

9 a They have completely smooth soles

10 b 23.77m (78ft)

11 a 0.914m (3ft)

12 c Centre line

13 c Seven

14 c Seven

15 a Tennis elbow

16 c Northern grip

17 b Five minutes

18 a Gyrospin

19 c Rush to the net

20 b A short, sharp punching motion

21 b Point at the ball

22 d Dropshot

23 a You have less reach

24 c Backhand smash

25 b Lots of short side steps

26 a Foot fault

27 c Centre mark

28 d Steel

29 b Pronation

30 a A serve that your opponent fails to touch with his racket

QUIZ ANSWERS:

28 **Which of the following is NOT a recognized tennis court surface?**

a Clay

b Acrylic

c Artificial grass

d Steel

29 **What is the term used when you twist your wrist downwards as you serve?**

a Donation

b Pronation

c Coronation

d Play Station

30 **What is an ace?**

a A serve that your opponent fails to touch with his racket

b A serve that goes into the net

c A really hard serve

d A playing card with seven hearts on it

GLOSSARY

Ace
A winning serve that an opponent is unable to even touch with his racket.

Advantage
If the score reaches deuce (i.e. 40–40) then the next player to win a point gets an advantage.

Advantage court
The advantage court is the right-hand half of an opponent's court (as you are facing him).

Approach shot
The shot played before a player rushes to the net.

ATP
The Association of Tennis Professionals. The governing body of men's professional tennis across the world.

Backhand
A shot played when the back of your hand faces the ball (i.e. on the left-hand side of your body if you are right-handed, or on the right-hand side if you are left-handed).

Backspin
Spin that causes the ball to rotate backwards, achieved by slicing under the ball as you hit it.

Ball boy/ball girl
Tournament assistants who collect stray balls in between points.

Ball machine
A machine that fires balls out of a tube and lets players practise tennis on their own.

Baseline
The line along the back boundary of the court.

Centre mark
The short line that marks the centre of the baseline.

Cross court
A shot played diagonally across the court.

Deuce
The name of the score when the players have reached 40–40.

Deuce court
The deuce court is the left-hand half of an opponent's court (as you are facing him).

Double fault
When both serves fail to go in and the player loses the point.

Doubles
Tennis between two teams of two players.

Down the line
A shot played down one side of the court parallel to the tramlines.

Drop shot
A shot that barely crosses the net, lands very short and forces an opponent to sprint to the net to play it.

Eastern grip
The grip used to play a basic forehand. This grip got its name from the USA, where the courts on the east coast were, for many years, mainly made of grass and needed a grip that would allow the player to reach the low bouncing shots.

Fault
A serve that does not go in.

Foot fault
Before a player hits his serve, if his foot touches the baseline or the inside of the court, then it is a foot fault and does not count.

Forehand
A shot played when the palm of your hand faces the ball (i.e. on the right-hand side of your body if you are right-handed, or on the left-hand side if are left-handed).

Game
At the start of each game a new player serves. The game is over when one player (or doubles team) wins four points and is at least two points ahead of his (or their) opponent(s).

Grand Slam
Any one of the four major tennis tournaments around the world: the Australian Open in Melbourne; the French Open in Paris; Wimbledon in London; the US Open in New York.

Ground stroke
A shot played from the back of the court after the ball has bounced.

Half-volley
A shot played immediately after the ball has bounced and before it has had time to rise up from the ground.

Intercepting
A term to describe when one player in a doubles team reaches across and takes a shot which his partner was in a better position to play.

ITF
The International Tennis Federation. The governing body in charge of international tennis.

Let
An occasion when players decide to replay the point in the interests of fairness, when they are unsure if the ball was in or out, or if a serve goes in but clips the net first.

Line judge
The tournament official who decides whether balls land in or out of court.

Lob
A high shot played over an opponent's head while he is in the net position.

Love
A tennis scoring term meaning zero. The word possibly comes from the French word 'l'oeuf', meaning 'egg', because an egg is the same shape as a zero.

Love game
A game where one player (or doubles team) fails to score a single point.

LTA
The Lawn Tennis Association. The governing body of tennis in Great Britain.

Match
A competitive game of tennis normally won when one player (or doubles team) wins the best of three or five sets.

Match point
The point played when one player (or doubles team) needs just one more point to win the whole match.

Mixed doubles
Doubles tennis between two teams consisting of one male and one female player.

Passing shot
A shot which passes low and to the side of an opponent while he is standing at the net.

Rally
A sequence of shots played between players during a point.

Referee
The head official at a tournament who is in charge of all the umpires and line judges.

Seeds
The top players in a tournament, who are given special positions in a draw to ensure they don't play one another early on in the tournament.

Semi-western grip
The grip used to hit high bouncing balls with a lot of topspin. This grip got its name from the USA where the courts on the west coast were mainly hard, requiring a grip that enabled players to reach the high-bouncing shots.

Service
The shot played by one player from behind the baseline which starts off each point.

Set
A set is a group of games and is won when one player (or doubles team) has won six games, by a margin of at least two games over the opponent(s).

Set point
The point played when one player (or doubles team) needs just one more point to win the set.

Sideline
Another word for tramline.

Singles
Tennis between two solo players.

Singles sticks
The sticks used in singles tennis to raise the net slightly at each end. In doubles tennis the singles sticks are removed so that players can play shots down the sidelines more easily.

Slice
A shot played by slicing the racket under the ball and giving it backspin.

Smash
A high ball hit above the head with power into an opponent's court.

Stop volley
A volley that takes the speed off an opponent's shot and causes the ball to drop short into his court.

String savers
Small pieces of plastic positioned where the strings cross one another. These help to prolong the life of racket strings.

Strings
The cord with which the ball is hit. It is stretched across the head of the racket.

Sweet spot
The area around the centre of the strings that allows players to hit a good, clean shot.

Tennis elbow
A painful injury in the elbow caused by vibration in the racket, a wrong-sized grip or poor techniuue.

Tie-break
A long game played at six games all in which both players, or doubles teams, serve. The first player or team to win seven points (by a margin of at least two points) wins the tiebreak and therefore the set.

Topspin
Spin caused when a player brings the racket up and over the ball as he hits it, causing it to rotate forwards.

Tramline
The thin strip that runs down each side of a singles court and is only used for doubles tennis.

Umpire
A tournament official who sits on a high chair at the side of the court making sure that match scores are always correct and that the rules are enforced.

Unforced error
A point lost because of a mistake rather than an opponent's good play.

Vibration dampener
A small piece of rubber tucked at the bottom of the racket's strings, used to prevent annoying vibration when the ball is struck.

Volley
A shot played before the ball bounces.

Western grip
A grip used to hit the ball with lots and lots of topspin. This grip got its name years ago from the USA, where the courts on the west coast were mainly hard and needed a grip that enabled players to reach the high-bouncing shots.

WTA
The Women's Tennis Association

INDEX

ACKNOWLEDGEMENTS

Hamlyn would very much like to thank all those at **Manydown Tennis** and **The Queen's Club** for the use of their facilities, as well as the following players:

Brian Farrelly
Rachael Crowther
Charlotte Crowther
Peter Hale
Ashley Armstrong
Jay Samuda
Jake Nicholls
Sue Nicholls
Rosie Brown
Michael Gilks
Hannah Swanscoe
Ian Griffin
Matthew Gordon
Rebecca Chetwood

Many thanks are also due to **Jane Bowen** at the LTA.

The drills are taken from the LTA coaching department manual *Game Based Practices*, by **Daniel Thorp and Jonathan Pankhurst**.

Copy editor **Adam Ward**
Proof reader **Nina Sharman**
Index **Indexing Specialists**
Senior Designer **Peter Burt**
Designers **Les Needham and Ginny Zeal**
Picture research **Christine Junemann**
Production controller **Lucy Woodhead**

Illustrations **Kevin Jones Associates**

All photography by **OCTOPUS PUBLISHING GROUP LTD**/**Gerard Brown**, except for the following:
ALLSPORT/**Brian Bahr** 26; /**Gary M. Prior** 34-35, 53, 60, 106; /**Clive Brunskill** 6, 14 top right, 28-29, 30-31, 66, 94, 104; /**Stuart Forster** 14 bottom left, 52, 62, 108 top; /**Hulton Getty** 12, 13, 33; /**Stuart Milligan** 11; /**Ezra Shaw** 10, 82; **COLORSPORT**/**Morris** 27; **DUNLOP SLAZENGER GROUP** 20, 21 Top, 21 Bottom, 22

```
80025 75540
```